ALTERNATIVE PLEASURES

Alternative Pleasures

POSTREALIST FICTION
AND THE TRADITION

Philip Stevick

UNIVERSITY OF ILLINOIS PRESS
Urbana, Chicago, London

LIBRARY OF CONGRESS CATALOGING IN PUBLICATION DATA

Stevick, Philip.
  Alternative pleasures.

  Includes index.
  1. American fiction—20th century—Criticism and
interpretation—Addresses, essays, lectures. I. Title.
II. Title: Postrealist fiction and the tradition.
PS379.S74   813'.54'09   80–25900
ISBN 0-252-00877-4

FOR TERENCE, THOMAS, AND JANE

Contents
Contents

Preface

THIS IS A DIFFERENT BOOK, not because I have sought, out of perversity, to make it eccentric, although I can be as perverse or eccentric as anybody, but because I have come to the subject of recent unconventional fiction in my own way and that way, I discover, is not exactly anybody else's.

One way of making a book about recent fiction is to make a frame concept and then write a first chapter, asserting that one's frame concept defines the novelty of new fiction. Then one makes a canon consisting of several writers who seem to bear out one's frame concept, writing applied chapters about each one of them in turn. I have not done that because the moment I imagine a frame, it turns into a Procrustean bed. And the moment I try to construct a canon, it crumbles and cracks before my own skeptical eye.

I find that I write most easily and profitably about new fiction when I allow myself to cite a range of writers, some of whom may not be widely known, some of whom may work in minor forms, and some of whom may well be less than great. It simply happens to be an age, in my opinion, containing an enormous amount of talent and great imaginative energy, but not a canonical body of dominant fiction.

If the writers of fiction in the seventies form a pyramid, it is a pyramid without a peak.

I also find that I write most easily and profitably about new fiction when I allow what I have to say to organize itself according to certain modes, themes, and images, and it will be obvious to the reader that that is what I have done in this book.

What else I have done is less obvious. The phrase "traditional fiction" by now means very little: the tradition of prose fiction since Cervantes includes *Tristram Shandy* and *Père Goriot, Vanity Fair* and *The Egoist, Tom Sawyer* and *The Ambassadors*. Still, the body of fiction from the seventeenth to the mid-twentieth century, however broad in its techniques and its stance before "the world," does present a group of possibilities or norms. And although those norms are very broad, they are finite. One recognizes Uncle Toby affectionately releasing the fly out of the window as one of the things that fiction can do, just as one accords that same recognition to Balzac rendering a grocer on a specific date on a specific street in Paris.

I have tried to measure the modes of recent fiction I have isolated against those norms within the tradition that seem pertinent, partly because I think imprecise and exaggerated claims have been made for the apparent break with tradition that new fiction seems to present, partly because I believe, with Carl Becker, that "Historical-mindedness is so much a preconception of modern thought that we can identify a particular thing only by pointing to the various things it successively was before it became that particular thing which it will presently cease to be." What has resulted is a series of approaches to new fiction, a group of ways in which it can be apprehended, known, and experienced, both in itself and in reference to the continuity of its genre.

Mine is a different book but not a corrective or a revisionist one. There is scarcely anyone to correct. It strikes me as amazing that, for all the critical activity in modern American life, there is so little critical writing on recent fiction. Even scholars and aficionados of Joyce, Lawrence, and Beckett must agree that there is a kind of insane redundancy in the enormous commentary appended to them. It is time we took some of the mind and wit at our disposal and tried to understand some of the very good fictions being written now.

Everything I cite in my book I enjoy. Some postrealist or postmodernist or experimental or new fiction seems to be crudely done, self-indulgent, and ephemeral; some seems to me, in ways I cannot define, repulsive and not of my world. But the works that I point to, and many more that I do not, have moved me, made me laugh, puzzled me, and given me what that old voluptuary Nabokov called "aesthetic bliss." I invite the reader to disagree with my constructs if he wishes, but I implore him to believe that I have written about recent innovative fiction not as an object to be studied but as something that I have loved.

The following chapters have appeared previously in different, sometimes considerably altered, form: chapter 1 as "Metaphors for the Novel" in *TriQuarterly* 30 (Spring 1974); chapter 4 as "Other People: Social Texture in the Post-War Novel" in *Missouri Review* 1 (Spring 1978); chapter 6 as "Naive Narration: Classic to Post-Modern" in *Modern Fiction Studies* 23 (1977–78); chapter 7 as "Lies, Fictions, and Mock-Facts" in *Western Humanities Review* 30 (1976); and chapter 9 as "Prolegomena to the Study of Fictional *Dreck*" in *Comic Relief: Humor in Contemporary American Literature*, ed. Sarah Blacher Cohen (Urbana: University of Illinois Press, 1978). A portion of chapter 3 appeared in the essay "Scheherezade Runs out of Plots, Goes on Talking; The King, Puzzled, Listens: An Essay on New Fiction" in *TriQuarterly* 26 (Winter 1973); a portion of chapter 5 in "Sentimentality and Classic Fiction" in *Mosaic* 4 (1971); and some of chapter 8 in "A Note on Satire without an Object" in *Scholia Satyrica* 1 (Summer 1975). I am grateful to the editors for permission to reprint this material.

I am also grateful to Temple University for the study leave during which this book was begun and for various forms of released time as it was being completed.

ALTERNATIVE PLEASURES

CHAPTER ONE

Metaphors for the Novel

AMONG THE MOST MEMORABLE LINES in modern poetry are those that offer a metaphor for poetry itself. Readers who could not remember another line by Archibald MacLeish can remember that poetry is a fruit. And readers with no particular taste for Marianne Moore can recall fondly that poetry is a garden, with toads. It is a classic impulse, making metaphors for poetry, and it appears from time to time in the poetry of all periods. Probably the poet most given to making metaphors for poetry was Keats and an entire book exists to comment upon Keats's various comparisons, that poetry is a woman, that poetry is a drug, and so on. It is significant that metaphors for poetry generally occur in poems, rarely in prose discussions of poetry. The fact establishes their special character: metaphors for poetry have, themselves, a kind of lyric status, existing in an "as if" world, highly individual, highly charged with linguistic complexity, ambiguity, nuance. As for the other arts, most of us would be hard pressed to think of a single memorable metaphor for architecture, say, or sculpture. The art of fiction, however, has stimulated a range of metaphors of extraordinary virtuosity and great seriousness.

Such metaphors for fiction are at least as interesting as those for poetry. And, unlike the metaphors for poetry, metaphors for the novel occur in every rhetorical situation, both in and out of fictive works, sometimes as heavily charged with wit and ambiguity as the cleverest metaphor about poetry, sometimes quite lumpish and programmatic. At times transformations in the art of the novel have turned upon metaphors. Certainly transformations in the way we read novels have turned upon metaphors.

The first thing to do with metaphors for the novel is to collect them; the second is to make sense of them. Providing attributions tends to limit our thought about them. To take a single example, if we recall that Fielding said the novel was an epic, then the power of Fielding's metaphor is reduced by our attribution. Calling a novel an epic is likely to seem to us a very time-bound thing to do, involved with Fielding's own attitudes toward literary hierarchies, attitudes that we no longer share, involved with Fielding's establishment of a noble lineage for his novels, half-seriously, half-ironically, a lineage that is not likely to interest us any more. If we withhold attribution, however, and simply list Fielding's metaphor along with somebody else's, a copywriter, say, for a middlebrow publishing house, then the metaphors can do their work, free from the historical condescension we are apt to give to Fielding and free of the aesthetic condescension we are apt to give to the copywriter, who may, for all of the wrong reasons, have happened upon a perfectly luminous trope for the art of fiction.

Here, detached from context, is my own list.

> A novel is a machine.
> A novel is a dream.
> A novel is a polemical tract.
> A novel is a *cri de coeur*.

A novel is a photograph.
A novel is a prayer.
A novel is a river.
A novel is a game.
A novel is a baby.
A novel is a bomb.
A novel is a labyrinth.
A novel is a poem.
A novel is a play.
A novel is an essay.
A novel is a diagram.
A novel is a sermon.
A novel is a therapeutic act.
A novel is an act of political aggression.
A novel is an act of coitus.
A novel is an act of masturbation.
A novel is an act of ritual.
A novel is a phonograph record.
A novel is a house.
A novel is a mirror.
A novel is a lamp.
A novel is a dance.
A novel is a musical composition.
A novel is a map.
A novel is a living body.
A novel is a dead body.
A novel is an act of vision.
A novel is an act of speaking.
A novel is an autopsy.
A novel is a feast.
A novel is a passenger train.
A novel is a painting.
A novel is a movie.
A novel is a scientific experiment.
A novel is a world.

A novel is a puppet show.
A novel is a high-wire act.
A novel is a book.
A novel is a newspaper.
A novel is an encyclopedia.
A novel is a history.
A novel is a suicide note.
A novel is fingernails on a blackboard.
A novel is a pudding.

The easiest way to begin sorting out the metaphors is by attending to motive. Fielding's motives I have alluded to. Let Fielding's apparent motives stand for a consistent motive among writers, readers, and critics of the novel from the origins of the genre to the beginning of the twentieth century, the wish to confer dignity upon the genre by offering comparisons with objects that we regard highly and, in so doing, to direct our attention to those aspects of the novel in which the novel shares all of the power and craft of those cultural objects that seem at the time to be indisputably great. To be sure, this defensive maneuver differs from period to period—from the eighteenth century, when the novel was in need of defense as a latecomer among genres, to the early twentieth century, when the novel, then preeminent among genres for a century and a half, seemed to need defense against the narrowness of its audience and the rarefication of its art or against the apparent moribundity of its classic forms.

Of course the vehicles of such defensive metaphors shift, also, according to the cultural assumptions of their times. That is, in a period in which the novel is found to be morally trivial if not morally salacious, one can counter, as Richardson and his partisans did, by calling the novel a sermon. In an age in which the novel is found to be a facile entertainment, lacking in rigor and precision, one can counter, as Zola and the naturalists did, by calling the novel a scientific experiment. In an age in which the novel is found to be heavy, didactic, and documentary, one can counter, as Thackeray did in a gesture at once ironically self-deprecatory and triumphant, by calling the novel a puppet show. In an age in which the novel is understood atomistically and shallowly, one can counter, as James did, by calling the novel a living body.

Strange things happen when we detach these metaphors from their highly specific historical situations. Is every novel in some permanent sense a puppet show, even the most dogged and fact-ridden novel one can think of, *Germinal*, for example? Of course it is, though probably not in the sense Thackeray intended his metaphor to carry for his own book. Is there some sense in which every novel is a scientific experiment, even a novel that is visionary and fantastic? Is *Alice in Wonderland* a scientific experiment? The use of metaphor as a cultural defense of the novel is out of fashion at the present time for one obvious reason: it is necessary to defend only what is attacked and, although the fiction of the seventies is widely ignored, it is rarely attacked.

Besides the wish to confer dignity and importance upon the novel, there is the wish, carried forward by metaphor, to correct what one takes to be a prevailing misapprehension. Consider the power of metaphor as a tool of revisionist theory in the hands of F. R. Leavis and the *Scrutiny* critics. "The novel is a dramatic poem," they wrote, and those of us who can no longer remember what they said about *Wuthering Heights* or *Hard Times* can recall that, for them, the novel was a dramatic poem and should be read like one, in aggressive defiance of prevailing critical method. It is hard to see how the phenomenologists could function without revisionist metaphors, insisting as they do that a novel is not simply a form or an aesthetic object but an extension of consciousness, which is to say an act of vision, an act of coitus, a dream, a *cri de coeur*. And in recent years, the revisionist wish that we attend to the novel not as an ethereal cluster of disembodied effects but as a printed book held in the hand has been carried forward by its own family of metaphors.

All of these motives have a positive intent. It is certainly possible to invent a metaphor that supports a pejorative intent, separating other people's novels, popular novels, old-fashioned novels, from the kind that one likes or writes oneself. The novel is a pudding. Not all novels, of course. Only bad novels.

It is also possible to invent a metaphor which borrows authority from the whole genre by asserting that what happens in a special case is true of the whole of fiction. The novel is a musical composition. Some novels do have remarkable musical affinities, of course; *Point Counterpoint* and *Doctor Faustus* come to mind. In some sense any novel can be said to share certain qualities with music. If one wishes to advance the fortunes of the kind of novel that is intentionally "musical," one can employ the metaphor that will connect musicality with the consistent purposes of fiction in all times and places. The novel is a musical composition. Or the novelist who feels that his own novels perform for him a certain therapeutic function can shore up his own aesthetic by asserting that all novels are exercises in self-therapy. And, to some extent, all novels are.

Such shifting back and forth between the general and the particular suggests a common characteristic of most critical discussions of the nature of the novel, whether such discussion centers around a metaphor or not; and that is the likelihood that the word *novel*, intentionally or not, will be allowed to mean, variously, the whole genre, as it is understood by conventional historians of literature and described in histories of the novel, an abstracted and idealized continuity within the whole genre, using the word *novel* so as to include, for example, the refinements of James but exclude the crudities of Captain Marryat, and finally a single text or a group of closely related texts. "The novel," writes Lawrence, "is the one bright book of life." It is not clear from that sentence, not even particularly clear from the whole discourse within which it appears, whether Lawrence means the novel as a genre from Defoe to his own time, certain possibilities within the historical genre, or only certain potentialities within the form of the novel exploited mainly by Lawrence's own fiction. Of our list, take the well-known metaphor comparing a novel to a world. It is frequently not clear whether the person who uses the metaphor wishes to say that all novels are worlds, that it is the nature of the novel to be a world, or whether he only wishes to say that a few special novels, such as those of Dickens, create a world.

It is finally possible, speaking of motives, to make a metaphor as a kind of exercise in provocation, as an irony, in which the terms of the comparison are not at all clear, deliberately so, inviting us to interpret at a number of levels, finding complexity in the local works in question, complexity in ourselves, complexity in the entire genre of prose fiction, where we had previously found simplicity. The novel is a machine, writes Sterne, or rather Tristram Shandy, in what is surely the most unmechanistic novel ever written. Is it a total and transparent irony, asking us to see through Tristram and discover how unmechanical *Tristram Shandy* is? Is it a comment on the self-generating effect of fiction, the principle that things set in motion, within a novel, follow their own laws, generate their own energy, run their own course? Does the metaphor point not so much to the people and events within a fiction, as they generate their own energy, but to the author and his lack of control, Tristram's machinelike book being rather

like Charlie Chaplin's assembly line in *Modern Times*? Is
the metaphor really concerned with the conventions of
Sterne's book, its use of familiar bits and pieces so as to
make a functioning whole? Is the metaphor connected in
some way to the intellectual history of its time, a body of
thought in which the image of the machine plays a small
but highly significant part? Surely it is not presumptuous
to project onto Sterne the wish to confound and provoke
us with a metaphor for which more than one interpretation
is a legitimate one.

Puzzling over Sterne's metaphor suggests a further ambiguity of such metaphors, the capacity of at least some of
them to mean three quite different things, as they are
taken to refer to the creative act of the author, the work
itself, or the experience of the reader. Saying that the novel
is a house means that the making of a novel is in some ways
like the act of a carpenter or an architect, that the novel
itself is like an integrated set of functioning rooms, and that
the reading of the novel is like experiencing the organized
space of a building. Saying that the novel is a game means
that the composition is a playful activity circumscribed by
certain arbitrary rules, that the novel itself is in certain
ways autotelic, the source of its own laws, a repository of
"fun," and that the reading of the novel is like learning the
rules of, then playing, a game. Saying that the novel is a
therapeutic act means that the writing of it offers therapy
for the writer, that the novel itself is an aesthetic rendering
of a health-bestowing process regardless of writer and
reader, and that the experience of the novel is a potentially
sanative experience for the reader himself. It undoubtedly
often happens that the inventor of a metaphor will think of
it in one of its three possible senses and realize, only after
it has gained currency, that it can be used, is even being
widely interpreted, in one or two other ways.

Besides the motives of their inventors, metaphors for the

novel can be sorted out according to their primary focus of reference. The most obvious of these is the reference to another aesthetic object: a novel is a painting; a novel is a movie. Whatever the motive, such a metaphor has the effect of confirming and intensifying our sense of the artistic status of the novel. Conversely, a metaphor may refer to an area of experience or an object that is deliberately not aesthetic and whose comparative value seems to detract from the artistic status of the novel: the novel is a newspaper; the novel is a scientific experiment. For a genre that ordinarily appeals to a mass public, there is some tactical advantage in such a metaphor, since it seems to claim that, unlike poetry, painting, and symphonic music, which tend to be esoteric, fiction tends to be exoteric. There is the further tactical advantage of deliberately vulgarizing the novel, removing it from the class associations of the other arts with their salons, galleries, patrons, and limited circulation magazines, placing it instead in the area of the visceral, the physical, the quotidian, and the deliberately classless. Perhaps the most curious focus of reference is to extensions of the person, simple acts or gestures that are essentially private: a novel is a prayer; a novel is an act of coitus; a novel is an act of vision; a novel is a suicide note. All art is an extension of the person; but the family of metaphors that apply to the novel seem not to refer to the general exertion of the creative will upon the plastic materials of one's medium, as with the other arts, but to point instead to a special subjective exposure or a special *in-extremis* quality with which the extension of the person is invested, for which the agony of Flaubert can stand as exemplary. Finally, the focus of reference in such metaphors may be to an object or process that is seen kinetically, as a force, so that our attention is directed toward an effect upon recipients: a novel is a bomb; a novel is a passenger train; a novel is a polemical tract. Part of the reason for the existence of such metaphors is undoubtedly that the novel is a commercial product, whose force upon a potential audience must always be asserted by those who could wish that audience to buy it. It is also true that the force of a novel is inevitably diffuse, since one experiences it over a sustained period of days, and for that reason there is a certain utility in having the power of a novel compressed and represented in a single trope.

Just why this multifunctional, relentless metaphor-making should exist is hard to say, in any final way. It is clear, however, that criticism of the novel means two things: it means sustained, deliberate, analytical discourse, of which there has been, until the last two decades, rather little, and it means a fluid body of phrase-making, stance-taking, attitudinizing, and categorizing, of which there has been, from the beginnings of the novel, a very great deal and of which the metaphor-making process is central. It is clear that the novel has served an institutional function more potent than that of any other genre during the last two hundred years and that this institutional primacy has permitted an enormous group of people with different training, interests, and sophistication to speak their minds on it: authors themselves, critics, casual reviewers, editors and publishers, clergymen, teachers, politicians, and ordinary readers who would not dream of speaking their minds on any other literary form. It is also clear that the novel, as a genre, is a loose assemblage of extremely diverse works and that at any given time since the middle of the eighteenth century there has always been a plentiful number of writers practicing *kinds* of fiction different from what one conceives to be the center of the tradition, a situation inviting the spiteful derogation of one's opponents with a dismissive metaphor, or the elevation of one's own kind with an honorific metaphor. And it is finally clear that the novel, being prosaic, invites critical rubrics that insist upon the wit, the imagination, and the verbal power of both the critic and the novelist, who is never so prosaic, such criticism tells us, as the surface of his prose would make him seem.

What has happened to such metaphors as the dominance of the modernists has given way to the fiction of the present time is: first, the enterprise has diminished, as polemical stance-taking has seemed less necessary than it used to be; second, certain metaphors that seemed to be permanently attached to the nature of the novel have ceased to be useful or even true of recent fiction; and third, a few metaphors, for obvious tactical reasons, have come to prevail over a large body of quite diverse fiction.

There have always been static novels—Clarissa moves only a few times and Jane Austen's contentment with her few square inches of ivory is legendary; but so many novels have arranged their events around travel, from adventure to adventure, from country to city, from home to "away," from class to class, that those metaphors indicating movement have always seemed central to the novel's purposes: the novel is a river, a passenger train, a map, a mirror on a road. It is hard to imagine a time when nobody will wish to read another novel that shows a transition from province to city, class to class, place to place, and novels that structure themselves upon an axis of physical movement are still being written, some of them with skill and insight. But the metaphor is dead: nobody, not even the writers and readers of such novels, would now say that the novel is a river or a train. As Raymond Olderman maintains in *Beyond the Wasteland*, the novel of the sixties projects a basically static individual as he interacts with basically static institutions, and the movement of such fiction is incidental, a description that seems to me to apply equally to most of the fiction of the seventies.

Metaphors that attempt to borrow the authority of fact—

the novel is a scientific experiment, the novel is an encyclopedia—are no longer useful since, despite the wave of
interest in the convergence of fiction and journalism, nobody really believes that fiction is dignified or definable by
its fact-bearing qualities. Those metaphors that point toward a kinetic relationship with the reader—the novel is a
bomb, a polemical tract, a sermon—all seem curious relics
of another time. And, of the metaphors that make a comparison with another art, only the comparison of novel to
movie or photograph seems to have any vitality. Yet, for all
of the obsolescence of many of the classic metaphors, a few
figures, as old as the novel itself, survive, in altered senses
perhaps but with undiminished power. The novel is a
world, Butor argues, thereby meaning to suggest the rendering of the consciousness of complex, interrelated space
characteristic of extended fiction. Butor's emphasis is different from the emphasis we might give if we were explaining the metaphor as it has been applied to Dickens or Jane
Austen, but it is by no means exclusive of those older ap-
plications. For, despite differences of emphasis, there is a
remarkable continuity that unites some very old ways of
understanding the novel with some new ways by the use of
that rich and durable metaphor. William Gass's *Fiction and
the Figures of Life* is surely the best repository of such
surviving metaphors: in a tone unmistakably of our time,
he argues that the novel is, for many readers, still a history,
for himself a voice, a poem, a world, a game.

The novel is a game. If we try to hold in the mind some
representative recent fiction—*City Life*, *Breakfast of
Champions*, *The Blood Oranges*, *Gravity's Rainbow*—
what seems to unite them is an autotelic, nonreferential
quality in which the value of the fiction inheres in its invention, its wit and intricacy of texture, its appeal as a
made thing, obedient to no laws but its own. It is the nature of critical metaphors that they be reductionist. If a

figure encourages us to see the autotelic qualities of a body of fiction, it thereby encourages us to overlook the extent to which such fiction is critical and engaged. If a figure encourages us to see the wit and play of a body of fiction, it encourages us to ignore the agony and despair. Still, it is not balance and judiciousness one wants from a metaphor but insight. Fiction in the seventies is dream, prayer, *cri de coeur*, and fingernails on a blackboard. But preeminently, as Fielding, Sterne, and Jane Austen knew, the novel is a game.

CHAPTER TWO

Form, Antiform, and Neoform:
Verbal Collage

Verbal Collage
Form, Antiform, and Neoform:

IMPLICIT IN THE IDEAS of fictional form current in every period is a set of counter ideas, or, if not ideas, impulses, that complicate ideas of form by asserting ideas of antiform. Fielding, for example, defined fictional form by analogy with historical form; he obviously believed in his analogy and to some extent fulfilled it; yet he consistently mocked the formula, writing novels, finally, that are not very much like the models of historical writing he and his readers knew. Fielding also made large claims for ideas of organic form long before the phrase became widely used, defining fictional form by reference to transcendent aesthetic categories such as unity, contrast, proportion, coherence, and consistent relevance to the general design. Yet he permitted himself to write such chapter titles as "A discourse between the poet and player; of no other use in this history, but to divert the reader" or "Containing little more than a few odd Observations." Fielding was more aware than most novelists since his time of the relation of concept to counterconcept. And part of the pleasure of reading him derives

from watching the splendid self-irony with which he plays
off the conviction that he has discovered the nature of the
thing he is doing against the equal but antithetical conviction that the thing he is doing is forever escaping his description of it.

Every novel, merely by virtue of its constant contact
with the amplitude and multifariousness of daily experience, contains material tangential or even antithetical to its
apparent formal principles, whether those formal principles are stated by the author, assumed by the readers, or
formulated after the fact by critics. Yet it is customary for
writers and critics to suppress a sense of the contradictoriness of prose fiction, assuming, for purposes of description,
that it is a much more constricted art than it is. Neither
Dickens nor his readers or critics have ever quite come to
terms with the vast number of different things that happen
in *Bleak House*, some of which surely escape even the most
comprehensive statement of that novel's formal principles.
And even works that strike us as pursuing aesthetic unity
much more relentlessly than Dickens ever did—*Madame
Bovary*, for example—contain material not altogether relevant to any formulable statement of their form. No one
would wish away Charles Bovary's cap, in the first chapter
of *Madame Bovary*. But the mimetic premises of Flaubert's
novel leave the reader quite unprepared for that grotesque
effusion, as if Flaubert had permitted the imagination of
Gogol to intrude into his second page. And the rhythms of
that novel, its allocation of interest and its solicitation of
our sympathy, insofar as these can be abstracted from the
novel, intellectualized, and put into words, provide us with
no justification for that strange but wonderful paragraph.

Certain works of the modernist period do display within
themselves a recognition of the contrasting claims of form
and the simultaneous wish to violate form. *The Counterfeiters* is an example of one kind. Again and again in the

Notebooks, Gide writes that the intention of his novel, indeed the very imperatives of fictional form at the time of his writing, compel him to do one thing; yet almost against his will the very passage he has just written and upon which he comments in his *Notebooks* does something else. "It can be said of almost all 'rules of life' that it would be wiser to take the opposite course than to follow them."[1] Joyce's *Ulysses* is the clearest example in English, though an example of a much different kind from Gide's, of the contrast between the two claims—to define form, to contemplate form, to pursue formal control, to take formal imperatives with such seriousness that the design of the novel becomes a veritable synthesis of narrative history, and to permit clutter, mess, muddle, trivia, the false lead, the unexplainable event, the irrelevant detail. It has been a commonplace of Joyce criticism almost since the appearance of *Ulysses* that countless local details appear in the book not because of formal demands but because they existed in *Thom's Official Directory* of 1905. And it has been a commonplace of Joyce criticism that the Man in the MacIntosh is a figure full of portent, a motif promising incremental meaning, a structural device promising symbolic reference, but that the Man in the MacIntosh is finally devoid of significance, a nullity, meaning anything or nothing, a device, as I would put it, of antiform. True to his idea of the nature of fiction, true to the particular architectonics of his novel, Joyce was also true to Dublin, and Dublin, not being organized according to aesthetic principles, compelled the inclusion of details that, even now, after half a century of obsessive Joyce scholarship, confound the expositors.

[1] André Gide, *The Counterfeiters* (New York: Modern Library, 1951), p. 450.

Recent fiction, in a remarkable number of cases, rather than suppressing the principle of antiform, extends the implicit examples of Gide and Joyce and the earlier examples of Fielding and Sterne by embracing it. The best-known passage of Barthelme's *Snow White*, for example, is the questionnaire that Barthelme inserts into the middle of his book. "1. Do you like the story so far? Yes ( ) No ( ) 2. Does Snow White resemble the Snow White you remember? Yes ( ) No ( ) . . . 5. In the further development of the story, would you like to see more emotion ( ) or less emotion ( )?"[2] *Snow White* is a strange and unpredictable book. Yet, however one apprehends its form, a questionnaire is not intrinsic to it. Other novels *assimilate* diverse materials. Perhaps it would be possible to say that even *Ulysses* finally assimilates all of its clutter and trash to its highly formulaic whole. But the questionnaire is not assimilated into *Snow White*. It is simply, perversely, there.

In lesser known books, versions of the same impulse appear. The snips and scraps of Charles Newman's *The Promisekeeper* or Constance Urdang's *Natural History*, for example—newspaper articles in narrow-column format, graffiti, handbills, signs, and diagrams—are not exactly assimilated, like realistic detail in Balzac, or like Joyce's clutter. Their appearance is perverse and discontinuous. In a different way, Stanley Elkin's *The Making of Ashenden* and Don DeLillo's *End Zone* change their formal premises as they go, not merely evolving as many traditional novels do, but transforming themselves into something not implicit in their beginnings. The first begins with the self-congratulatory reflections of an affluent, overrefined, almost Jamesean character and ends with his copulation with a bear. The second begins with an account of a football team in an East Texas college and ends as a meditation on global politics

[2](New York: Bantam, 1968), p. 82.

and eschatology. The most stunning examples of the embracing of formal contrariety are in the short fiction of John Barth in *Lost in the Funhouse*. Variously, within the same fictions—stories "about" Ambrose and his family; love and death; the life and times of the Eastern shore in the 40s; the technique of writing codified by a naïf; the technique of writing agonizingly faced by Barth; the relationship between print and reader; the relationship between pleasure and pain; the possibilities of continuity, coherence, and form; the vitality of narration; and the exhaustion of narration—they embrace, like nothing in prose fiction since Sterne and nothing except Sterne, the principle of formal perversity.

What I am beginning to describe is a narrative art far more audacious than the kind for which Dos Passos and others have borrowed the term *montage* from the art of the film. A French word meaning, roughly, *editing*, it has taken on an uncommon power, partly because of the associations the word has come to have with Eisenstein's great *Potemkin*, partly because of the theoretical debates between Eisenstein and Pudovkin concerning the nature and effect of sequence in film, partly because, whatever Eisenstein said or did, there *is* something uncanny and mysterious about the way in which the mind perceives the relationship between shots in a film.

Clearly Flaubert, in the scene at the agricultural fair in *Madame Bovary*, cuts, edits, or makes a montage with his unmodulated movement from the auctioneer selling swine, to Emma and Rodolphe professing love, even though there were no motion pictures to teach him how to arrange that scene. Anachronistically describing Flaubert's technique as a montage tells us something important about his art because it reminds us—all of us being initiates in the experience of film—of the way in which Flaubert structures and implicitly comments by the sequence of his "shots." Yet

Flaubert's scene or, to choose the most obvious example from the period of film, the newsreel section of Dos Passos's *U.S.A.* uses discontinuities in the service of continuities. Both passages carry forward an unmistakable sense of thematic selectivity; and what they begin to be, they become. For all of the audacity in its movement from shot to shot, one cannot imagine *Potemkin* containing, apropos of nothing in particular, a brief sequence showing a camel, a moving van, a rising soufflé. For all of the audacity in its movement from auction to Emma, one cannot imagine Flaubert's extended scene including, apropos of nothing in particular, a brief account of the climate of Tierra del Fuego. And, for all of the audacity in its movement from one news event to another, one cannot imagine Dos Passos including, apropos of nothing in particular, a description of a man sleeping.

Going beyond the fictional techniques that can be named by analogy with montage, the fiction I describe goes to exactly that point at which the violation of the implicit formal premises of a work by apparently antithetical elements becomes, in fact, normative. If what seem antiformal elements do become normative and take over the work, what we have is a new kind of form, one for which Aristotelean descriptions will not apply. Such fiction is not likely to have a beginning, a middle, and an end. It is not likely to fulfill long-term expectations. And it is not likely to structure itself, in any valid sense, upon a plot. As so often happens when the descriptive terminology of one art suddenly seems deficient, it is natural and useful to begin to reconstruct a terminology by borrowing from the description of another art—not film this time, useful as montage was for a time, but from the graphic arts. It is a move which, in this case, carries the authority of Barthelme.

In an interview the interviewer quotes an earlier sentence of Barthelme's, in which he says that "The principle of collage is the central principle of all art in the twentieth century in all media." Would he expand on that sentence? asks the interviewer. "I was probably wrong," replies Barthelme, "or too general. I point out however that New York City is or can be regarded as a collage, as opposed to, say, a tribal village in which all of the huts are the same hut duplicated. The point of collage is that unlike things are stuck together to make, in the best case, a new reality. This new reality, in the best case, may be or imply a comment on the other reality from which it came, and may be also much else. It's an *itself*, if it's successful: Harold Rosenberg's 'anxious object,' which does not know whether it's a work of art or a pile of junk."[3] It is one of the perils of the use of collage as an analogy, as Barthelme illustrates, that it expands so as to seem to include almost everything. New York is a collage. Fiction is a collage. The top of one's desk is a collage. The contents of one's pockets is a collage. Still, the analogy persists in the criticism of recent fiction, not merely because Barthelme used it but because it is a usable start in the restructuring of formal description.

Techniques that might, with some justification, be called collage have, of course, been around for a long time. *Anatomy of Melancholy* is an assemblage of one kind, and in our century, portions of *The Waste Land* and the *Cantos* are assemblages of another kind. American literature of the twentieth century sometimes shows the impulse to assemble. Evan Connell's *Points for a Compass Rose* is a splendid gathering of bits and pieces; Paul Metcalf's *Genoa* splices together fictive-autobiographical material from contemporary experience, materials from Melville's life, the words of his fiction, the words of his critics, the words of Columbus, bits of geographical and navigational information. And Agee, in *Let Us Now Praise Famous Men*, wishes

[3] Joe David Bellamy, *The New Fiction: Interviews with Innovative American Writers* (Urbana: University of Illinois Press, 1974), pp. 51–52.

that instead of describing the clothing of a sharecropper's family, he could paste a shoe itself into the text, an impulse to collage that, at that point, transcends words altogether. But all of these earlier acts of assemblage either declare themselves marginal and eccentric, as Connell's certainly does, or their acts of assemblage exist to serve larger purposes. Clearly the analogy *verbal collage* seems most appropriate when it names a fictional technique that is central to the aesthetic motives of its period and when the principle of assemblage is, radically and irreducibly, the principle of the whole work.

Just as clearly, the analogy verbal collage means something rather different from those modernist techniques so brilliantly discussed by Joseph Frank as "spatial form."[4] The intersecting simultaneities of *Ulysses* and the transcendence of time in Proust do result, no doubt, as Frank argues they do, in the kind of spatialization of literature that he names, a replacement of the sequentiality that has always been assumed to be of the nature of literature by the nonsequential sense of design that has always been assumed to be of the nature of the visual arts. Still, nobody would call *Swann's Way* a verbal collage. For, despite the transmutation of narrative into something that begins to resemble painting in its spatial effect, the images and events of Proust's novel are still apprehensible as elements of a linear design, continuous and coherent.

The principle of collage does seem to be clearly the case in Barthelme's story "The Party." "I went to a party and corrected a pronunciation," the story begins.

> The man whose voice I had adjusted fell back into the kitchen. I praised a Bonnard. It was not a Bonnard. My new glasses, I explained, and I'm terribly sorry, but significant variations elude me, vodka exhausts me, I was young

[4]"Spatial Form in Modern Literature," *Sewanee Review* 53 (1945):221–40, 433–56, 643–53.

once, essential services are being maintained. Drums, drums, drums, outside the windows. I thought that if I could persuade you to say "no," then my own responsibility would be limited, or changed, another sort of life would be possible, different from the life we had previously, somewhat skeptically, enjoyed together. But you had wandered off into another room, testing the effect on members of the audience of your ruffled blouse, your long magenta skirt. Giant hands, black, thick with fur, reaching in through the windows. Yes, it was King Kong, back in action, and all of the guests uttered loud exclamations of fatigue and disgust, examining the situation in the light of their own needs and emotions, hoping that the ape was real or papier-mache according to their temperaments, or wondering whether other excitements were possible out in the crisp, white night.

"Did you see him?"

"Let us pray."

The important tasks of a society are often entrusted to people who have fatal flaws. Of course we tried hard, it was intelligent to do so, extraordinary efforts were routine. . . . Zest is not fun for everybody. I am aware that roles change. Kong himself is now adjunct professor of art history at Rutgers, co-author of a text on tomb sculpture; if he chooses to come to a party through the window he is simply trying to make himself interesting.[5]

I have argued for a progression in which fiction has moved from a willing acceptance of a certain antiformal perversity to a new arrangement in which the undermining of the ostensible formal premises of a work become no longer perverse intrusions but norms. Still, judging from Barthelme's story, the collage that results is far from either a willed randomness or a kind of arty detachment from experience, mere word games, design for its own sake. However startling its movements from sentence to sentence and image to image, Barthelme's story begins to lay out a

[5] *Sadness* (New York: Bantam, 1974), pp. 57–58.

series of motifs and antitheses rather more controlled and less random than the continuity of a realistic art story—for example its alternation between references to energy and zest on the one hand and to fatigue and boredom on the other; or its modulations between the domestic interior within which the party takes place and the "outside"; or in its modulation among at least three levels of cultural experience, the level of impersonal officialese, the level of personal encounter, and the level of the intersection of person and mass culture. Far from being random, Barthelme's collage is also far from being pure design. What it seeks to be, I think, and what it seems to be for most readers is a stylized and intensified version of parties, those parties being, in experience, of the nature of collage—disjointed, fragmentary, full of social formulas, chic tastes, and ritual phrases. In that sense, the principle of collage curiously serves the classic function of mimetic art by devising a structural vehicle that indicates the rhythms, the feeling tone, and the perceived content of the experience itself.

Visual collage can be made of anything, chair caning, egg shells, rusty nails, paint, ticket stubs; and the finished composition need not suggest anything about the areas of experience from which those assembled objects came. *Verbal collage*, on the other hand, can only be made successfully of those scraps that belong to areas of experience which seem to be collages already—a commercial strip of urban roadway, an evening of television, a recollection of a political campaign, a large party. Visual objects do not carry with them the same organizational imperatives that words do. A piece of chair caning and a ticket stub, placed beside each other, "mean" nothing because no prior value determines that they should be perceived in any relation to each other. Syntax, rhetorical order, and linear narration, however, *are* prior imperatives; and, thus, if they are violated, their violation will seem purposefully expressive of disorder.

Structurally, a visual collage implies these principles. First, implicit in the enterprise is the wish to make textural shifts, moving from paint, to cloth, to pasted paper, to wicker, to cemented, three-dimensional objects. Second, implicit in the enterprise is a wish to make the most of a certain interplay between the hidden and the manifest. In realist painting, to be sure, as in experience, objects are concealed behind other objects. In a picture containing a sunset, however, the sun, although receding behind a hill, would not be spoken of as being *hidden* by the hill. In a Rauschenberg collage, on the other hand, one recognizes a replica of a newsprint photograph of John Kennedy, hidden in part by the willful superimposition of other elements of the composition. So it is with visual collage in general. We do not see scraps and fragments but whole artistic gestures such as parallel paint marks, overlapping as it were, so that each element appears as a recognizable whole, partly obscured by the overlapping effect of one or more adjacent elements. Third, implicit in the enterprise is a wish to move tonally between elements that are serious and elements that are frivolous, elements that seem to belong to the realm of pure aesthetic—nonsignificant shapes and paint marks—and elements that are chosen to seem especially quotidian, scraps from a newspaper, theater tickets, found objects. Fourth, implicit in the enterprise is a wish to make a gestalt out of objects that, by their nature, would seem to be irreconcilable, disparate, and totally heterogeneous, making them, by a sheer force of the aesthetic imagination, into a whole.

Barthelme's "The Party" does present structural rhythms for which existing literary description is plainly inapplicable and for which the analogy of collage is both an apt descriptive tool and an enabling fact of aesthetic history, since without the rich possibilities exploited by the visual media "The Party" would not have come to exist. Nothing in fictional theory prepares us for that movement in the story toward the sentence "Drums, drums, drums, outside the windows," a sentence suggestive both of one of the forgettable clichés of B movies of the forties and of the not altogether fanciful imagination of an apocalyptic tribal life beyond the apartment in which the party takes place. The rhythms of collage plainly do describe that narrative movement, not simply in the abruptness of the shift but also in the textural difference in moving from the bureaucratese of the sentence before it to the overcivilized, personal analysis of the sentence following.

For those characteristic shifts between the elements of collage, shifts at once of subject matter, tone, style, and relation to experience, I suggest the word *juncture*. In a visual collage, one is always aware of its junctures because one takes in the composition as a whole and every part insists upon its willed, pasted, juxtaposed quality. In a verbal collage, on the other hand, the junctures must be frequent enough to keep us aware of its mode of composition, since a verbal collage is experienced sequentially. The early sections of Waugh's *A Handful of Dust* are remarkably discontinuous. But each section is some pages long. And thus the remarkable absence of transition that marks the movement from section to section in Waugh's novel occurs at wide intervals, spaced between continuous passages of conventional narration; and, although the effect is disconcerting, it is not of the nature of collage. This suggests a principle: the most audacious and startling junctures can occur in a fiction without that fiction seeming unconventional; the degree to which a fiction seems of the nature of collage will seem, more than the result of any other force, directly proportional to the frequency of the juncture. Among contemporary novels, for example, Evan Connell's

Mrs. Bridge makes a stark juncture between each section, those sections being generally between one and three pages. The effect is of a scrapbook, perhaps, but not a collage. It is a wonderful novel, rich, wise, witty, and intricately observed. But it does not seem to occupy the same ground with clearly postmodernist novels. Renata Adler's *Speedboat* makes a juncture at the end of nearly every paragraph, which is to say that almost no two consecutive paragraphs are "about" the same events or even tap the same cultural level with the same stylistic and tonal resources. If for no other reason than the rhythms of its junctures, it seems technically postmodernist, although less relentlessly and audaciously so than Barthelme's "The Party." Different purposes are being served and different sensibilities are on display in the fiction of Jerzy Kosinski, Leonard Michaels, Walter Abish, and Ronald Sukenick. But all of these, and many more, find a common usefulness in the manipulation of comparably unmodulated movements.

To make a fiction, we have always thought, is to tell a story, although we have learned that one can tell it from the inside or the outside, backward or forward, implicitly or directly, with a set of stylistic resources that is self-consistent or mixed and various. What is now obvious is that one can make a fiction not by telling a story at all but by a verbal activity that is analogous to cutting and pasting. What the eighteenth-century novelists knew and acknowledged, and what the nineteenth-century novelists knew and suppressed, is that, having begun to tell a story, one allows, necessarily, a certain latitude of effect and a certain range of inclusiveness that sooner or later violates the implicit principles of the story one began to tell. What certain fiction of our own time proposes is a form in which the violations of principle are perpetual, the form continually redefined, so that discontinuity is the norm and linearity is superseded by the arrangement of fragments. What is important, however, is less the discovery of the formal possibility than the discovery of its power. For, as Pynchon's monumental collages surely demonstrate, the result of cutting and pasting, far from being a mere exercise in arrangement, becomes, as does fiction in all times and places that finds its own formal ways to its own vision, a way of knowing.

CHAPTER THREE

The Feel of the World

OF COURSE RECENT POSTREALISTIC FICTION gives shape
to a different sensibility from that of the dominant modernists. To draw the comparison more finely, it gives shape to
a different sensibility from that of the dominant American
novelists of the fifties, still largely realistic in their presen-
tational conventions and modernist in their assumptions
about the nature of their craft, inheritors of the legacy of
Joyce and Lawrence, Faulkner and Hemingway. If the
word *sensibility* seems quaint, let us agree that recent
postrealistic fiction gives shape to a new consciousness of
the world, new sources of energy, delight, and sensual joy,
new areas of pathos, new sources of the comic. There are
two ways of attempting to take the measure of this new
consciousness of the world. One is to find a fixed point,
outside of fiction itself, that tells us what the world is like,
so we can let that philosophical insight organize the fiction
for us. The other way is to attempt to get inside the fiction
with as little intellectual baggage as possible. It is the second that seems to me the more responsible. The world,
somebody says, is now so complicated that anything one

says about it is true. If it is the fiction one is interested in, one had better trust the vision of the fiction.

I begin with a passage obviously intended to be dense, rich, and evocative, carefully made, self-conscious, but solidly of the late modernist period, unmistakably *before* the work of the postrealist, postmodernist writers who are my subject. Jean Stafford's "A Country Love Story" begins in this way:

> An antique sleigh stood in the yard, snow after snow banked up against its eroded runners. Here and there upon the bleached and splintery seat were wisps of horsehair and scraps of the black leather that had once upholstered it. It bore, with all its jovial curves, an air not so much of desuetude as of slowed-down dash, as if weary horses, unable to go another step, had at last stopped here. The sleigh had come with the house. The former owner, a gifted businesswoman from Castine who bought old houses and sold them again with all their pitfalls still intact, had said when she was showing them the place, "A picturesque detail, I think," and, waving it away, had turned to the well, which, with enthusiasm and at considerable length, she had said had never gone dry. Actually, May and Daniel had found the detail more distracting than picturesque, so nearly kin was it to outdoor arts and crafts.[1]

The most conspicuous feature of the passage, if one is thinking of obvious contrasts with the experimental fiction of our own decade, is the treatment of time and physical objects. "An antique sleigh," "snow after snow," "eroded runners," phrases like these from the first sentence begin to present a durational mode that is little short of obsessive, projecting us immediately into a world of waiting, expecting, contemplating, appreciating, hoping, wondering, all of those experiences in which the mind and the sensibility are deployed around the central object of the con-

[1] *The Collected Stories* (New York: Farrar, Straus & Giroux, 1969), p. 133.

templation, slow change. Both objects and people bear with them the marks of their own past; everything decays and disintegrates; both nature and people present the appearance of cyclic or ritualistically recurring behavior. In addition, time, in that passage and in such fiction in general, always carries with it an implicit valuation. A character shows his age gracefully or clumsily; the process of aging carries with it great dignity or great pathos; an aging object carries with it a sense of decreased value, as a result of its diminished usefulness, or a sense of enhanced value, as a result of its tasteful durability. And so it is that we are unsure, in that first paragraph, whether the sleigh is worn out, and should be discarded, or is an authentic antique, and should be preserved. There is no doubt that the cyclic, ritualistic house-buying and -selling of the "gifted business-woman" is specious and faintly repulsive.

It need hardly be said that no one goes through life with his eye so firmly fixed on the clock as this, saying to himself, A is older than B, but B bears its age more gracefully than A. Such an obsession with time is a convention which we never particularly noticed as a convention when a great deal of fiction was written in that way. Yet, stylized and conventionalized though it may have been, such an obsession with time in modernist fiction surely represents a mode of perceiving the world and feeling its rhythms, shared, in a more diffuse and less specialized way, by the general culture.

Furthermore, Jean Stafford's paragraph evokes a set of relationships between two different modes of existence, in this case the man-made object and the forces of the natural world, and these relationships are played upon in a symbolic way. The function of a sleigh is to ride in the snow, not to be covered by it. And we know, even from the first sentence, that the presence of the sleigh, immobile and nonfunctional, will be made into a metaphor, charged with a flexible, ironic value, a metaphor for the presence of man in the world. As in the case of time, such a man-nature dichotomy, as a center for a symbolic charge of meaning, is a convention, present in the kind of sensibility fiction that Jean Stafford represents. In fact, it is a device central to innumerable novelists in the nineteenth century, such as the Brontës, Dickens, and Hardy. A Romantic way of focusing one's consciousness of the world, that man-nature dichotomy is a familiar device both of fiction and the general culture for a hundred years.

Moreover, there is, in Jean Stafford's story, the presence of the thing itself, an object pulled out of the background and conspicuously placed before our attention, described from a double viewpoint, near and far, given a touch of the pathetic fallacy (the sleigh has "jovial curves"), and above all invested with taste. The sleigh, of course, is a chameleon image and is in good taste or bad according to its human context. And it is a marvelously versatile structural device, which compresses and gathers together a number of attitudes axial to the story that follows. But there is not much doubt that the image of the sleigh is more than a trope or a structural device to Jean Stafford and her readers. It is a *thing*, with intricacy of contour, complexity of texture, solidity, and the marks of its own past. Whatever its usefulness in the story, it is an image that issues from the imagination of a writer fascinated with the material objects of daily, sensory existence, a mode of understanding central to Anglo-American fiction from Defoe to what survives of the realistic tradition in the present time.

As a point of contrast, I suggest three beginnings antipodal to Jean Stafford's. The first fiction of Donald Barthelme's *City Life* begins:

An aristocrat was riding down the street in his carriage.
He ran over my father.

* * *

After the ceremony I walked back to the city. I was trying
to think of the reason my father had died. Then I remembered: he was run over by a carriage.[2]

Robert Coover begins his fiction "A Pedestrian Accident"
in this way:

Paul stepped off the curb and got hit by a truck. He
didn't know what it was that hit him at first, but now, here
on his back, under the truck, there could be no doubt. Is it
me? he wondered. Have I walked the earth and come here?

Just as he was struck, and while still tumbling in front of
the truck and then under the wheels, in a kind of funhouse
gambado of pain and terror, he had thought: this has happened before. His neck had sprung, there was a sudden
flash of light and a blaze roaring up in the back of his head.
The hot—almost fragrant—pain: that was new. It was the
place he felt he'd returned to.[3]

Ursule Molinaro's "Chiaroscuro: A treatment of light &
shade" begins:

She first noticed the bump on Sunday morning. Her first
Sunday in the art critic's elaborate downtown apartment. 3
days after she'd moved in with him.

On a Thursday, when she always did things; when things
always seemed to happen in her life. When she'd finally let
the art critic convince her to move out of her parents' house
& in with him. After convincing her that living with one's
parents was living with one's past, when one was past 20.[4]

Certain common qualities of method, voice, and sensibility unite the three beginnings, different as they are from
each other. But against the background of Jean Stafford's
story, what is most remarkable is their extraordinary distance from her prose. They simply do not register the same

[2]"Views of My Father Weeping," *City Life* (New York: Bantam, 1971),
p. 3.
[3]*Pricksongs & Descants* (New York: Dutton, 1969), p. 183.
[4]*TriQuarterly* 29 (Winter 1974):41.

world. That obsessive sense of slow change, of cyclic movement, of the growth, maturation, and antiquity of the ob-
servable data of the world that seems so necessary to the
experience of Jean Stafford's world is either absent altogether or oddly transmuted. Barthelme's opening is almost
atemporal: sketchy, indifferent to age and change, reminiscent of the rhythms of fable and myth. Coover's opening is
atemporal in a different way, recounting an event for which
a finely divided, acutely observed sense of time is simply
irrelevant. Ursule Molinaro's opening puts us rather ner-
vously in contact with the calendar and the main character's age, but it is all curiously distant, detached from cause
and effect, values good or bad, any density of human context. It is impossible to imagine Jean Stafford saying, of a
character, that things happened to her on Thursday. The
resonant movement between human and nonhuman that
gives so much energy to the beginning of Jean Stafford's
story is absent in the three beginnings I cite, suggesting
that the old Romantic convention is no longer of use in a
fiction in which the made and the born, the authentic and
the schlock, the natural and the manufactured are all taken
as the given data of a difficult world that simply cannot be
divided into halves. As for the material texture of the fiction, the affectionate regard for things that is obviously so
important to Jean Stafford, one recalls that the narrator's
father, in Barthelme's tale, is run over by "a carriage." The
carriage is driven by "an aristocrat." Paul, in Coover's fiction, does see and feel with painful acuity. But he is in no
position to show much interest in the texture of things.
And Ursule Molinaro's beginning presents us, by Jean Stafford's standards, with a stupefying vagueness: "the bump,"
"the art critic's elaborate downtown apartment."

The points of contrast between Jean Stafford's story and
new fiction are almost limitless. Take the phenomenal set-
tings, for a further example, the ways in which the charac-

ters' conscious experience is controlled by the spaces in which the authors choose to present it. Jean Stafford's story begins in a front yard, but its energy and attention are directed toward a house. In due course certain exterior events will take place, but the characters' most intense emotional scenes are lived out within rooms. It is not merely a convenience of staging, to place the characters within those spaces in which they most conveniently interact. And it is not merely the realistic result of the fact that the characters, being upper middle class, do spend most of their time in rooms. There is an obsessive, housebound quality in such fiction, reminiscent of Samuel Richardson, in which doors and windows, corridors and stairs, beds, tables, and chairs all figure heavily. There was a time when it seemed that that was simply the way very much fiction was written, with characters condemned to work out their fates in studies, kitchens, and living rooms. But once again, new fiction presents a remarkable break with that convention. Ursule Molinaro's fiction, it is true, begins with a transition from one interior space to another. But neither one is rendered or felt, either in the passage I quote or later in the story. Generally, in the fiction I am beginning to describe, the physical space that encloses the consciousness of the action is undefined, nonspecific, in some vaguely hallucinatory way, or extreme, artificially constricted perhaps, or unaccountably open, or visionary, in which the contours of physical space are heavily shaped by the experiencing mind. If the action in a new fiction does take place in houses, it is never for purposes of defining the usualness of a cast of domestic characters or for rendering the roombound effect so useful to Jean Stafford.

Or consider the way in which the stylistic orientation of the fiction makes concrete its epistemic orientations. Take the preciousness of Jean Stafford's phrase "an air not so much of desuetude as of slowed-down dash." Why *desue-*

tude? Why not *disuse*? Consider the *as-if* clause that follows. That single sentence contains the effect of two principles, one a movement toward elegance when directness
would seem to interfere in the wit and flair of the phrase,
the other a movement toward embellishment in the interests of demonstrating an imagination expansively and lei-
surely at work upon its materials, comparing, supposing,
qualifying, conjuring alternatives, musing. It goes without
saying that the as-if clause, as a syntactic strategy, does not
exist in new fiction. The as-if clause seems to imply that
the empirical reality being described is rather bizarre, sufficiently unfamiliar so that some conjectural cause must be
supplied to account whimsically for its being so bizarre.
The writer of new fiction does not know why empirical reality is as bizarre as it is. He does know that the stylistic
patterns which render the introspective, contemplative,
domestic imagination of the fiction of the fifties are un-
available to him. And the alternative is a style rather stark
and plain, often naïve, terribly vulnerable, about which I
will have more to say.

Let us turn the comparison the other way, to those things
that new fiction seems to be doing, that late modernist fiction seems ill equipped to do. I suggest, of my three examples, their pervasive sense of the body. Each of the
three presents pain, physical embarrassment, an especially
agonizing sense of what it feels like to inhabit one's skin.
People in new fiction itch, hurt, bleed, look at themselves
in the mirror where deformities grow before their eyes,
walk quite a bit, and die.

Furthermore, each of the selections, and much more of
new fiction, *experiments*—if that is the word—with forms
of directness, a kind of awful abruptness, in which an
event, death, violent accident, inexplicable deformity that
must be led up to, explained, prepared for, or set in a context is, instead, simply told. The beginnings of the three

fictions are as striking as they are because they are more than simply violations of conventions—they are epistemic dislocations. The clearest analogue that I can think of is Kafka's great beginning, "As Gregor Samsa awoke one morning from a troubled dream, he found himself changed in his bed to some monstrous kind of vermin."

Each of my three selections suggests a nonspecific mythic resonance to its rather uncomplicated action. One recalls how labored, intricate, "serious," and willed are the mythic elements in most modernist fiction. Barthelme's story, with its aristocrat and coach, suggests some ancient and elemental tale. But it is hard to say whether that mythic dimension enriches the fiction, adding a layer of timeless human depth, or whether it detracts from its gravity, making it silly. Paul, in Coover's beginning, has "walked the earth and come here," an archetypal wanderer, now beneath a truck. Ursule Molinaro's character is, in some vaguely magical way, a victim of numbers and the calendar. Such mythic suggestions in new fiction consist of echoes, phrases, mimed bits—unelaborated, unsustained, dubious in their values. It would be uncharacteristic of postmodern fiction to develop consistent mythic parallels, as so many modernist works do. Joyce deploys over a very large book the ironic parallels of Stephen Dedalus as Telemachus, Bloom as Odysseus, and Molly as Penelope. But it is Joyce who imagines the parallels, not the characters, who do not fancy themselves incarnate myths. Leopold Bloom does not think that he is Odysseus; he thinks he is Leopold Bloom, advertising canvasser. Paul, on the other hand, does think, for a moment, in a passing phrase, that he is an archetypal wanderer. But it is hard to derive much significance from the idea, since he is flat on his back, beneath a truck.

Each of the three selections generates a comic sense very different from the late modernism of Jean Stafford and different from nearly anything within the modernist period. Jean Stafford's beginning is comic; the three characters shown are overcivilized but fallible, and that contrast, seen from the superior conspiracy of author and reader, is potentially comic. The characters are smart, clever, poised, articulate, graceful, and knowing; but they are also, at moments, foolish, coarse, and inept. And at such moments, we permit ourselves a silent amusement. The three pieces of postmodernist fiction I cite contain none of the wit that signals to us the ways in which we may feel the classic condescensions of comedy. The sense of the world for writers of new fiction embraces a sense of the comic that coexists more easily with pain, humiliation, bad taste, and impotence than we are accustomed to respond to. It is a sense of the comic that derives not at all from the dominant modernist figures such as Mann, Gide, and Joyce, or even Faulkner; rather it derives, if it derives at all, from Kafka and Céline. In my examples, that eccentric new sense of the comic has something to do with the authorial postures of the writers—innocent and naïve, flip, facile, in a manner reminiscent of a stand-up comic ("Then I remembered. . . ." "Is it me? he wondered." " . . . when she always did things."), but tender and vulnerable, slow to figure things out, the very antithesis of the dominant modernists. And it has something to do, to circle back on an earlier point, with body and bone, the relation between the human frame and the world.

It is probably by its structure that we are best equipped to recognize the difference between fiction that seems to be classic modernist and fiction that seems to be audacious or experimental in some distinctly new way. In Jean Stafford's story, the events consist of tensions made only partly overt, harsh words, misunderstandings. Any sharply exterior events clearly exist to figure forth the moral and psychological dynamics of the characters. Ultimately the story

ends with a kind of plateau of understanding toward which
the rest of the fiction has worked. *Epiphany* is too facile
and imprecise a word for what happens at the end of the
story. It is a moment both of resignation and of awesome
frustration in the face of the future, and any word, such as
epiphany, which implies sudden insight is misleading.
Still, the structure of the story is in the tradition of epiphany fiction, which is to say that it values the private and
the domestic over the public and the external, that it dem-
onstrates a belief in the possibility that an intuitive self-
knowledge can cut through accumulations of social ritual
and self-deception, a belief so firm that it permits the intuitive act to serve as dramatic end point and structural
principle, indeed as the very moral justification for the fiction.

It takes only a sentence or two of Barthelme, Coover,
and Molinaro to recognize how far they are from epiphanic
form. All three tend to find more interest in the public
than the private, in the external than the internal, in the
freakish and extreme than the middle range of experience.
Nothing in the beginnings of the three fictions points to or
seems to create the enabling conditions for the epiphanic
illumination. None of the three writers seems to have
much interest in such intuitive insights, perhaps not even
much belief that they exist. And thus we do not need to
read to the ends of the three fictions to know that their
structures are antithetical to what is the most conventionalized, imitated, standardized feature of modernist fiction,
especially shorter fiction, of the last generation, the epiphanic illumination, or, as in Jean Stafford, the self-gener-
ated plateau of understanding that transcends the plane of
social conventionality and habitual self-deception which
has made the self-understanding both possible and necessary.

As for the three examples, perhaps the best way to approach the question of their structure is to jettison the word *structure* altogether. Structure carries with it connotations of economy, symmetry, accountable proportion, organic form, whether we wish it to or not. If pressed, most of us could apply any of those connoted values to any well-known piece of modernist fiction, certainly to Jean Stafford's story, could construct a systematic analysis by means of which every event, every image, every word could be accounted for by aesthetic principles apparently derived from the work itself. I do not think that habit of mind is appropriate to the three examples and I do not think that relentlessness of method will carry us very far.

All three of our exemplary fictions extend themselves in ways that are more additive than dramatic or progressive. In the barest and still the best definition of *form*, Kenneth Burke writes, "*Form* in literature is an arousing and fulfillment of desires. A work has form in so far as one part of it leads a reader to anticipate another part, to be gratified by the sequence."[5] Basically, such "desires" in shorter fiction are of three kinds: problematic, psychological, and conventional. We have a problematic desire when we have a secret to be discovered during the course of the fiction, a relationship to be perceived, a motive to be revealed. When the problem is resolved our desire is "fulfilled." We have a psychological desire when we expect a mental process within the fiction to run its course, self-ignorance to proceed to self-knowledge, perhaps, or personal hostility to proceed to personal accommodation. When the psychological process is complete, when the character has come to know what we have expected he must know, then our desire is fulfilled. We have a conventional desire when we are led to expect events, devices, and tonal manipulations typical of the genre. Jean Stafford's story is full of such con-

[5]*Counterstatement* (Los Altos, Calif.: Hermes, 1953), p. 124.

ventional desires and fulfillments, the sophisticated mas-
tery of the characters alternating with their humiliation and
ineffectuality, the compassion of the author alternating
with her ironic distance, the diminuendo into generalized
pathos at the end, all of these being typical of the genre.

In our three exemplary fictions there is no problematic
desire, unless one responds to Ursule Molinaro's beginning
with a curiosity about the pathology of the bump. There is
nothing that we might *wish* to know, as a key to understanding the beginnings. In none of the three fictions is
there any interplay between the psychological desires the
reader might project into the fiction and the fulfillment of
them: the characters are constructs, types, quite deliberately devoid of inner life. What they know they gather by
bits and pieces. If they solve a problem, the solution becomes a new problem and nothing is gained. Needless to
say, the three fictions do not give us much in the way of
conventional form. An alternative to saying that the fictions
are formless, which sounds gratuitously pejorative, is to
extend the idea of form beyond the linear progression defined by Burke toward something more mosaic, concentric,
or circular, which is to say that the consciousness deployed
in new fiction, with its general absence of interest in the
formal rendering of intuitive change, in the movement toward insight, or in the accumulation of wisdom, leads easily and naturally to the collage form I have described in the
previous chapter.

Earlier I have written about how comparatively flat and
empty of material texture new fiction is, in comparison
with the thing-centered quality of fiction from Richardson
to the late modernists. The additive, collagelike form of
new fiction, by allowing itself a special freedom from the
compulsion to surround its elements with value, discovers,
in fact, a kind of positive joy in the act of assemblage. In
the fiction of Richardson the principle is most fully realized

and firmly established that the data of the fiction, its places, things, and events are phenomena rendered by Richardson as perceived by the characters, which means not only perceived but also valued. Everything in Richardson is worth something, to the person who sees it and reports it to us. So it has been with fiction ever since. To see in fiction is to rank, to prefer or to deprecate, to value. One way of attempting to break with such a compulsion to value is to experiment with point of view, as Dos Passos does, for example, in those passages of his fiction that are made to seem unselectively documentary, mechanically recorded as it were. Another way is to arrange the elements of the fiction serially or capriciously so that the mode of presentation undercuts the possibilities of conventional value, a very old technique that serves the exuberance of Rabelais, the irony of Swift, and the associative anarchy of Sterne. Beckett's fiction is the most fully realized and powerfully executed attempt in modernist literature to undercut the values implicit in syntax, in conventional arrangement, and in the very act of telling, all in the service of his nihilistic vision.

In new fiction, the nihilism is still there, since no structure of values has arisen to move into Beckett's vacuum. What is different is that fiction now has the luxury of taking for granted what the modernists had to demonstrate. A writer of new fiction no more needs now to strain to demonstrate the absurd than a Victorian novelist needed to strain to demonstrate a Christian-capitalist ethic. A peculiarly indirect way into the valueless surface I am describing is through the description by John Barth of the substance of Smollett's *Roderick Random*.

> Sailors, soldiers, fine gentlemen and ladies, whores, homosexuals, cardsharpers, fortune hunters, tradesmen of all description, clerics, fops, scholars, lunatics, highwaymen, peasants, and poets both male and female—they crowd a

stage that extends from Glasgow to Guinea, from Paris to
Paraguay, and among themselves perpetuate battles, de-
baucheries, swindles, shanghais, rescues, pranks, poems,
shipwrecks, heroisms, murders, and marriages. They wail
and guffaw, curse and sing, make love and foul their
breeches; in short they *live*, at a clip and with a brute *joie
de vivre* that our modern spirits can scarcely comprehend.[6]

Elsewhere in the same essay, Barth summarizes the import
of Smollett's novel:

In short, *Roderick Random* is *par excellence* a novel of nonsignificant surfaces—which is not to say it's a superficial,
insignificant novel, any more than the age that produced it,
the age that invented the English novel, was superficial or
insignificant.[7]

Consider the order of events, or rather the order of the
recollections, in the story by Barthelme I have used as a
model. Interspersed with interviews of witnesses, mother,
and perfect strangers are "views," as Barthelme puts it in
his title, of father. Father throws his ball of knitting in the
air. Father jams his thumb into the frosting of cupcakes on
a tray. Father pretends to be a burglar, with bandana and
water pistol. Father tries to ride a large dog. Father has
written on the wall with crayons. Father weeps. Father
shakes pepper into the sugar bowl. Father lies in bed.
Father looks in a mirror. Father looks through a door.
Father weeps. It is surely the most perverse and contrary
piece of father-reminiscence, or mock father-reminiscence,
ever written, those discontinuous snapshots of father as
static image, as naïf, as cut-up, interspersed with dreamlike passages purporting to investigate the accident in
which he dies.

Whatever else the story does, it assembles, gathers, cuts

[6]"Afterword," *The Adventures of Roderick Random* (New York: Signet,
1964), p. 478.
[7]Ibid., p. 471.

and pastes, without honorific heightening, without satiric undermining, like pictures in a scrapbook. Barthelme's pastiche is a vast distance from the bawdy gusto of Smollett, of course, but the effect is in some ways comparable, surfaces without depth and significance, taking their origin in a mixture of motives both perverse and joyful, with the result being an assemblage in which the individual elements, some of which are silly, some of which are inexplicable, and some of which are depressing, unmistakably convey the pleasure of the writer in his function as assembler.

It is more than a set of technical devices that I am describing, rather a way of seeing the world, and it appears in most writers who seem innovative. Compare a passage from Rudolph Wurlitzer's *Nog*:

> I ventured a peek out the door, but she had left the bedroom. I preferred to think she hadn't heard me; that, indeed, she had never heard me. I could still slip out. The terrycloth bathrobe was hanging behind the door. I put it on and turned to investigate the bathroom. It was a beautiful bathroom. There was a huge green tile tub, a new toilet and washbowl. I opened the cabinet over the washbowl. I couldn't stop looking at the objects on the top two shelves; suntan oil, Anacins, cold cream, three pink hair curlers, two yellow toothbrushes, one of which was very dirty, Dramamine pills, Itolson eye bath, Ban, Kolex cold capsules, Ammens Medicated Powder and a small box of Benzedrin pills. I stared at each object and then went over them again.[8]

Or consider a passage from the title story in William Gass's *In the Heart of the Heart of the Country*:

FINAL VITAL DATA

The Modern Homemakers' Demonstration Club, the Prairie Home Demonstration Club. The Night-outers' Home

[8](New York: Random House, 1968), p. 15.

Demonstration Club. The IOOF, FFF, VFW, WCTU,
WSCS, 4-H, 40 and 8, Psi Iota Chi, and PTA. The Boy and
Girl Scouts, Rainbows, Masons, Indians and Rebekah
Lodge. Also the Past Noble Grand Club of the Rebekah
Lodge. As well as the Moose and the Ladies of the Moose.
The Elks, the Eagles, the Jaynettes and the Eastern Star.
The Women's Literary Club, the Hobby Club, the Art
Club, the Sunshine Society, the Dorcas Society, the Pyth-
ian Sisters, the Pilgrim Youth Fellowship, the American
Legion, the American Legion Junior Auxiliary, the Gardez
Club, the Bridge for Fun Club, the What-can-you-do?
Club, the Get Together Club, the Coterie Club, the Worth-
while Club, the Let's Help Our Town Club, the No Name
Club, the Forget-me-not Club, the Merry-go-round
Club. . . .[9]

Or consider a passage from the third of my exemplary fictions, Ursule Molinaro's "Chiaroscuro":

She had a vision of her mother's ring-stripped hands
reaching across the Sunday breakfast table. Across 4 carefully separated stacks of Sunday papers:
The stack which had been read by her father, but not yet
by her mother. The stack which had been read by her
mother, but not yet by her father. The stack which had not
yet been read by either. & the stack which had been read
by both. On top of which sat her mother's fat black & white
cat. Formally erect, on top of the breakfast table.[10]

Not all new fiction is as joyously assembled as are these
passages, so fascinated with series and symmetry, variety,
and amplitude, so determined not to confer value. But
most new fiction shares, to some degree, the spirit of those
passages.

In an earlier chapter, I suggested that the most durable
metaphor for the novel, the one that expresses most point-
edly the condition of fiction at the present time, is the

[9](New York: Harper & Row, 1968), p. 198.
[10]*TriQuarterly* 29:43–44.

metaphor of game and play. Insofar as that metaphor is appropriate, it seems to deny the legitimacy of the analysis I have been conducting, an analysis that seeks to find common qualities of consciousness and sensibility in recent fiction. Either fiction is a game or it is an expressive vehicle—or so it would seem—not both. Of course a given work of art can serve many purposes, fulfill many motives, and "mean" in innumerable ways. But there does seem to be a special exclusivity between playing and finding ways of expressing our deepest feelings about the world. It is this exclusivity we point to when we say, of a person whose sincerity we doubt, that we think he is playing games.

Actually the game metaphor is likely to express several aspects of fiction now, none of which squares very easily with an expressive function: an antimimetic impulse, against realism and the visible world and against a verisimilar, or credible, rendering of the inner world; an autotelic, nonpragmatic aesthetic motive, in which fiction aspires to the condition of abstract painting or music, answerable only to itself; the cultivation of a range of verbal activities that place a high premium on nonpurposive ingenuity, activities that another period would have called cuteness, cleverness, mere facility, and worse; and the cultivation of a tacit pact in which reader and writer agree to suspend certain expectations about each other, out of a shared mistrust of old modes of literary high seriousness.

But art always finds ways of holding together irreconcilables: the erotic and the devotional, for example, the sublime and the trivial, the verbal and the ineffable. It is, perhaps, the best way of explaining the success of new fiction, when it succeeds, and its failure, when it fails. When it succeeds, it is as re-creative, clever, and autotelic as it can be while still preserving its expressive function. When it fails, it fails because that equipoise is lost, either on the side of a mere facility of arrangement, out of touch with the human, or on the side of a gloss of novelty overlaying a flat conventionality of mind.

A single sentence of Leonard Michaels's seems to me to contain the contrary pressures I have described in a kind of exquisite distillation. Technically it is a sentence no one could have written twenty years ago, not that it calls attention to itself as a piece of experimental prose, but simply that it must strike the reader as something different from the patterns of image and the rhythms of prose available to writers then. It must have been fun for Michaels to have made, and it is fun to read, with its eccentric periodicity, its visual rendering of the acts of the mind, its energy, its shocks to what is left of our sense of decorum, its final series. Experientially it catches hold of a terrible awareness of self and fixes it in cold print with the classic power of fiction always, in other times, in other places. "A sense of his life constituted of moments like this, inept and freakish, when spirit, muscle, and bone failed to levels less than thing, a black lump of time, flew out of his occipital cup like a flung clod and went streaming down the inside of his skull with the creepy feel of slapstick spills, twitches, flops, and farts of the mind."[11]

[11] *Going Places* (New York: Farrar, Straus and Giroux, 1969), p. 190.

CHAPTER FOUR

Other People

A HANDFUL OF LINES in modern literature hang in the mind with an awesome power that has something to do with their brevity and concentration, something to do with their resonance and their capacity to engage us at the level of what Lovejoy called "metaphysical pathos." One such sentence is "History is a nightmare from which I am trying to awake." No one who has heard it forgets it. Another is "Things fall apart,/ The center cannot hold." I suggest that one sentence which invites the persistent attention given to Joyce's great sentence on history is Sartre's line near the end of *No Exit*, "Hell is—other people!" It is an extraordinary sentence because of the art of its compression, the power of its irony, and the chill of its insight. But it is an extraordinary sentence for American readers because it reminds us of the special pathos that we are entitled to read into Sartre's universal principle. Radical individualism has always been our fate and our curse, and our characteristic sense of the world is often located somewhere between mere loneliness and full-blown paranoia. There is scarcely a novelist of consequence from Hawthorne to the present time who does not, sooner or later, in some of his charac-

teristic moods, join with Sartre's Garçin in deciding tha-
tother people are, indeed, hell. Perhaps the American sentence that most strikingly links Sartre's line to the vision of
our own postwar fiction is the sentence in Seymour Glass's
diary in *Raise High the Roofbeam, Carpenters,* "I have
scars on my hands from touching certain people."

That self-enclosed and defensive posture, so characteristically American, finds its own rhythms and conventions
in the fiction after the war. Those conventions of the fifties
and early sixties are, it goes without saying, never so limiting as they seem when one sets them down and describes
them. Novelists of that period press against their limits,
escape them altogether. And, to be sure, some novelists
even go on as if those conventions, by means of which
other people are customarily apprehended and set down in
a novel, simply do not apply to their kind of fiction. Still,
the conventions are there. Other people *are* hell, and
American novelists of the postwar period find their own
ways, to some extent shared and self-imitative, of saying so.

"Doctor Posmanture's hands were shaking so much the
thermometer kept rattling against Mrs. Tupperman's lower
teeth. Finally he got the silver tip under her tongue and
went to the window." I quote from *A Fine Madness* by Elliott Baker.[1] It is a skillful and engaging novel but not an
enduring one, and it reads now rather like a period piece,
which makes it all the more useful as a repository of the
conventional. Published in 1964, it extends and stylizes
certain patterns characteristic of the sensibility of the
fifties. One notices first, in the passage I quote, the presence of a trembling doctor. Doctors in fiction are always
emblematic, never more so than in postwar fiction. We
wish doctors both to cure us and to love us. In postwar

[1](New York: Putnam, 1964), p. 16.

fiction, doctors are prepared to do neither. Later, Baker-writes: "The web of her mind unraveled and lay waiting to be restrung. Before she could do it, the bedroom door opened, and Doctor Posmanture came in like a pall bearer." There is more to Dr. Posmanture but not much more: he advises patients without convincing them, he reflects on embarrassments and missed diagnoses past and present, he retreats when advanced upon, he trembles, and he looks like a pallbearer. It is fair to say that Doctor Posmanture is more than another quack doctor in a long comic tradition, more than a pusillanimous fool with a fool's name in a fool's body. He is an object of contempt, represented by the narrator of Baker's novel with such back-of-the-hand scorn that those few sentences I quote suffice to signal us that our antipathy is being solicited and we are being invited to loathe.

What Elliott Baker does with Dr. Posmanture is, in some respects, at least as old as what Fielding does with Thwackum and Square. In some respects it is very much of its time. Dr. Posmanture, in common with a large number of comic characters of other periods, is implicitly emblematic of a failed, or flawed, institution. Also in common with those classic comic characters, Posmanture carries with him a phonetic tag, in this case his last name, that confers upon him, in some mysterious, Dickensian way, the status of buffoon. Also, classically, he is a repository of what Erving Goffman calls "stigma symbols."[2] He visibly trembles. For a doctor with a thermmeter in his hand, the tremble is more than a descriptive detail; it is a sign, in Goffman's phrase, of a "spoiled identity." Finally, in classic fashion, his speech acts never wholly succeed. People do not pay attention to him when he speaks; if they do, they misunderstand his tone; if they understand his tone, they do not

[2] *Stigma: Notes on the Management of Spoiled Identity* (Englewood Cliffs, N.J.: Prentice-Hall, 1963), pp. 46–48.

believe what he says; or, if they do, they find him even when credible ridiculous.

What make him seem especially characteristic of the fiction of the fifties and early sixties are two qualities. First, the way in which Dr. Posmanture is apprehended by the speaker of the fiction, taken up by the eye, held in the consciousness, and deployed on the page for the reader to respond to—all of this is organized almost totally around matters of style, not substance. Thwackum and Square, Gradgrind and McChoakumchild, such classic characters *believe* things, and their style is continuous with their intellectual life. The comic characters in Twain and Faulkner are moral agents whose style is continuous with their moral life. But Posmanture has neither an intellectual nor a moral life: his style is all he has. Secondly, Posmanture exists in the whole of the novel as one variation in a simple bipolar arrangement. There is the self, in this case the narrator of the novel and his protagonist Samson Shillitoe, who are, together, the locus of energy, authenticity, and wit, and there is everybody else, all of them different in style but all of them equally fatuous, square, oafish, or menacing. The world of *A Fine Madness*, in other words, contains a hero and others, and those others are wall-to-wall, elbow-to-elbow Posmantures. Hell is other people.

Criticism of the fiction of the period I describe tends to submit to the rhetoric of that fiction, to accept its implicit values, and to locate the center of interest in the solitary figures who give each book its energy and its reason for being. It is largely proper and inevitable that criticism should do so. One picks up a passage of critical writing on *Catcher in the Rye*, for example, expecting it to be made up almost exclusively of assertions, mostly sympathetic, about Holden Caulfield, hardly imagining how it could be otherwise. What I mean to suggest, however, is that, at the

distance from those books at which we now stand, important things can be said about them, not by making assertions about Holden Caulfield, but by making assertions
about that social fabric which surrounds him and which he
refracts for us. I mean to suggest, further, that the social
fabric was more stylized and conventionalized than we ever
knew when it was the fiction we all read and believed in,
and that those conventions have now been abandoned both
because, like most conventions, they have a limited durability and because they represent a stance before the world
that nobody can now afford to celebrate.

Consider Miss Frost, one of Sebastian Dangerfield's sex-
ual partners in *The Gingerman*. Proper and reserved, as
her allegorical name suggests, she speaks in phrases such
as "Dear me" or "You're just going on," a monosyllabic dolt-
ishness counterpointed with the involuted verbal energy of
Dangerfield. She represents a failed Catholicism and a
mindless domesticity, talking about hell and mortal sin and
frying a sausage while Dangerfield nibbles her earlobe.
Physically she wears a gray sweater or a woolly robe; short
hairs grow from the sides of her head, and around her nose
the flesh turns up. It takes only a few details to begin to
suggest that structurally Miss Frost is akin to Baker's Posmanture, with her lumpish style, her institutional associations, and her place in the fabric of all those other people
whom Dangerfield gulls and despises.

Beyond those broad correspondences that link two such
different characters as Miss Frost and Dr. Posmanture, I
suggest a large and intricate iconography that served a significant segment of writers for a decade and a half as a way
of verifying the otherness of other people. Other people
tend to have flawed bodies, which are closely observed as
if in a photograph by Richard Avedon or Diane Arbus, with
teeth, hair, or facial features in some way apparently mis-

placed. Other people tend to wear shapeless or graceless
or tasteless clothing. Other people tend to hold object-
sawkwardly, often to drop them. Other people tend to have
vaguely comic names, usually foregrounded by an incan-
tatory repetition. (On two pages, Dangerfield says "Miss
Frost" seventeen times.) Other people tend to use words
literally and tonelessly. Other people tend to repeat a certain pointless motor activity, to gesture irrelevantly, to
twitch, shrug, or smile apropos of nothing. Other people
tend to have a special affinity for machines such as tele-
phones and televisions. Other people tend to have a special
affinity for pills, medicines, and patent preparations of the
more obvious and odorous kind. Other people tend to organize their speeches, and implicitly their values, around
cant words used as totems. What the novelist who manipu-
lates such an iconography does, in short, is to juxtapose
two frames (to borrow again from Goffman), one frame
within which the author, the hero, and the reader are assumed to be enclosed, containing a shared value system, a
shared set of behavioral norms, and a shared phenomenology, and a second frame in which other people are assumed
to be enclosed, in which all of the aspects of mind and body
are conspicuously more flat and more banal.

Charles Simmons's brilliant and largely neglected novel
Powdered Eggs, published in 1964, makes an extraordinarily useful transition between the mode of fiction I have
been describing and the possibilities that have followed it
in the decade since. It is, in some respects, continuous
with that fifties tradition, with an energetic, inventive,
iconoclastic narrator observing for us a passing gallery of
moral cripples, many of them institutional types, using a
method heavy with the physical tics and verbal gestures of
the people observed. In other respects, the novel, in common with the fiction of the seventies, extends and intensi-

fies that tradition delineated in Robert Alter's *Partial
Magic*,[3] a reflexive tradition extending from Cervantes
through Sterne and Diderot to Nabokov, Simmons's novel
being, in common with those older novelists and in common with Barthelme, Coover, and many more, arch and
self-aware about its own artifice, self-conscious about its
rhetoric. It ends, finally, with a passage that looks both
ways, to those moments in the second book of *Don Quixote*
in which the characters read the first book of *Don Quixote*
with wonder, fascination, skepticism, and irritation and to
those passages in Barth in which Barth's fiction holds itself
up to playful and ingenious self-scrutiny, namely a deroga-
tory review of *Powdered Eggs* by Charles Simmons. ("No-
where is there the slightest indication that the narrator's
attitudes differ from the author's. In fact, I suspect that this
is largely an autobiographical book, thrown together from
real letters the author wrote to a real friend. How else explain the book's inordinately abrupt and unpleasant jerki-
ness, or its accordion quality, which would seem to allow it
to be half as long as it is as well as twice as long?")[4]

Other people, through the eyes of Simmons's narrator,
can be as oafish, unfeeling, stupid, and repulsive as characters in any fifties novel, but a new note appears—of tenderness and vulnerability at times, at other times of compassion for perfect strangers—that few of those earlier
novels could have contained. At one point, the narrator
encounters three old ladies, "one in a wheel chair, two
pushing. Old, old ladies." They pass and he imagines the
rhythms of their lives, their human integrity, their satisfactions and lost opportunities, their loneliness. The passage
is sentimental, if one can use that word without its pejorative connotations. It is totally devoid of condescension.
And it is a remarkable gesture, one of many in the novel,

[3](Berkeley: University of California Press, 1975).
[4](New York: Dutton, 1964), pp. 219–20.

of openness and generosity toward unknown people. Simmons's novel is full of detestable characters. And for short passages, its sensibility seems comparable to that in Donleavy and Salinger, Ken Kesey, James Purdy, Jack Kerouac, Herbert Gold, the Updike of *Rabbit, Run*. But the Sartrean phrase finally does not fit. Other people are not hell because other people include three old ladies, "one in a wheel chair, two pushing."

The varieties of social texture in the fiction of the present decade are, in some sense, infinite. But they are also reducible, without much distortion, to the two modes which Simmons's novel prefigures. No one can now write a new *Gingerman*. What one can write is a fiction in which other people are all but irrelevant, in ways which earlier fiction anticipates but does not so fully realize, other people being subsumed by the intricaces of artifice for its own sake, eliminated in the interests of a radical solipsism or a narcissistic self-enclosure. Secondly, what one can write is a fiction that rediscovers ways of apprehending other people, a fiction aware of the burden of fifties fiction and aware as well of the logic of Barth's "Literature of Exhaustion," yet willing to find an atavistic energy, often an unreserved, sensual pleasure, in living in the world, different from anything in the decades before.

Some of the shorter fiction of Barth's provides the purest examples of the first of these possibilities, exercises in reflexiveness so sustained and total that other people cease to exist. The art of Barth has been widely and justly admired, but the development I describe has not been sufficiently remarked. Prose fiction could almost be defined as narrative that presents a sustained interaction between self and others. That others are rather less important in the texture of certain modernist art novels than in the classic realistic novels does not diminish the audacity of the ultimate development in Barth—a fiction so turned in on itself that it effectively eliminates others, leaving only the self. *The Universal Baseball Association* by Coover eliminates other people in the interests of another kind of purity, no less audacious than Barth's, in which a large cast of figures exist only in the mind of Henry Waugh and even those barflies and ne'er-do-wells who exist in the empirical world of the novel are assimilated into the network of relationships that exists only in Henry Waugh's head. If such a radical solipsism seems narrow and self-defeating, and in the long run it probably is, one need only reflect on the varieties of telling devised by the South Americans and the Europeans in the last twenty years—I mention three: *The Book of Imaginary Beings* by Borges, *Invisible Cities* by Calvino, and *Mobile* by Butor—that pursue ends which have nothing to do with the interaction of self and other but which are among the most brilliant and luminous fictions of our time, solipsistic and autotelic, yet at the same time life-enhancing.

Much of Barthelme seems to me to devise paradoxical ways of effectively eliminating other people from fictive situations in which the *presence* of other people appears to be the irreducible nature of that situation. Not much of Barthelme is reflexive monologue, in the manner of Barth, or solipsistic world, in the manner of Coover's Waugh, or self-enclosed invention, in the manner of Calvino or Borges. Barthelme is generally urban and social, the action taking place in cities, on streets, in apartments. For other people not to exist on "forty-five blocks north-south and an irregular area east-west" of Manhattan is a stunning stroke of the imagination. Yet in *The Balloon*, one of Barthelme's most charming inventions, other people are, by some perverse logic, both *there, en masse*, and negligible, abstract, and generalized to the vanishing point.

The balloon expands over several square miles of New

York City "while people were sleeping."[5] People agree that "the meaning of the balloon could never be known absolutely." Children jump and bounce on the balloon. Some people are hostile to the balloon; others are vexed because it is inexplicable; but large numbers of people feel toward the balloon a deep warmth. Various conclusions are possible about the balloon: one man might say this; another might think that. Ultimately people begin to locate themselves in relation to aspects of the balloon. People "turn, in bewildered inadequacy, to solutions for which the balloon may stand as a prototype, or 'rough draft.'" Finally the balloon is removed to West Virginia by "trailer trucks." So it is that, except for an excursus in the last paragraph in which the speaker refers directly to a woman whom he seems to love and who guesses that the balloon belongs to the speaker, the vast metropolitan response to the phenomenon is seen, understood, and recorded with the generalized jargon of bad sociology and intellectual posturing in general, all of the reactions to the balloon being collective and abstract, leaving the story without a proper name, a face, a body, or a genuine exchange of conversation. Barthelme's is a rich and various talent; and no doubt somewhere—perhaps between Edward and Pia, perhaps between Snow White and her leering dwarfs, not, I think, between the Dead Father and his children—an exchange between self and other can be found. But *The Balloon* is representative of considerable areas of Barthelme's imagination, an imagination with a chilling knack for discovering the modes of our anonymity, the diction of our impersonality, the patterns of our paranoia, the mind-set we absorb from our electronic media, our self-serving incantations, our manifold ways of transforming real people into general ideas, our ways, in short, of living in a world of people while denying them their unique otherness.

[5](New York: Farrar, Straus & Giroux, 1975), p. 5.

As for the second possibility I have named, the possibility not of eliminating other people but embracing them, the varieties are stunning and problematic, the problems lying not in the forms of the works, which tend to be intelligible, but in the sensibilities, which are likely to be puzzling to a reader trained in the hardness and dryness of the classic modernists. In John Gardner's *Nickel Mountain*, for example, the characters speak to each other in clichés. But rather than condescending to them or placing them at an ironic distance from himself, Gardner seems to display them with an implicit tenderness, as if they represent for him a communal and unselfconscious ease that his academic sophistication denies him. "'How's business, Slim?'" asks a trucker of the corpulent proprieter of the diner that serves as the main locus of the novel's action. "'Can't complain,'" the other replies. "'You?' 'Can't complain.' 'How's the wife?' 'Oh, not bad, not bad; about the same.'" Other people's bodies, the starting point for so much comic delineation in fifties novels, are often oddly shaped but apprehended with interest, an absence of scorn, often with affection, with an eye for family resemblances and a fondness for rendering the gestures of inarticulate tenderness. The professions, the object of so much contempt in fifties novels, are treated with a stylized respect, the doctor, for example, being a clever and sympathetic practitioner with a thin veneer of cynicism, known to his friends in the village as "Doc." And the novel organizes its most powerful effects around such fundamental human events as birth, marriage, and death more relentlessly than any novel since Agee's *Death in the Family*.

I do not wish to imply that *Nickel Mountain* represents the wave of the future, neither do I mean to overvalue its art. What I do mean to imply is that it represents one possibility for prose fiction in a world in which writers and readers share a sensibility much altered from that of two decades ago. Larry Woiwode's *Beyond the Bedroom Wall* begins: "Every night when I'm not able to sleep, when scrolls of words and formulas unfurl in my mind and faces of those I love, both living and dead, rise from the dark, accusing me of apathy, ambition, self-indulgence, neglect— all of their accusations just—and there's no hope of rest, I try again to retrace the street."[6] No one can know, from that first sentence, whether we are in something comparable to the world of *Nickel Mountain*, and no one can predict whether a country doctor will, in due course, appear. What one can know is that we are in touch with a sensibility that shares certain features with Gardner's, lyrical and evocative in its prose, humble and self-abasing, vulnerable, open, and confessional, above all *tender*, a word I use because I can find no suitable substitute.

The fiction I describe is full of echoes. It is like the fiction one thinks one has read before. It takes what is perhaps the ultimate risk for a writer of fiction, which is not the risk of an inopportune subject matter, the risk of an unfashionable mode, or the risk of technical failure, but the risk of banality, the risk of trying, in public—in cold print—to find one's emotional bearings with the resources of a plain, lyrical, confessional prose in an age of irony and artifice.

R. D. Skillings, in a story entitled "Two Stories I Never Finished," writes of a return to the hometown and an encounter with an almost forgotten girlfriend. It sounds like the donnée for a story in *Good Housekeeping*, except that the story appears in *Antaeus*, where the reader can make his choice between defense, superciliousness, and distance or identification, vulnerability, and sentiment.

> "I always used to be in love with you," I said, "when we were little."
> "I had a crush on you too," she said.

[6](New York: Farrar, Straus, & Giroux, 1975), p. 5.

I had a shock of amazement and another sensation, less pleasant, of having been blind. Still, here we were.

"I hate to do this to you," she said, "but I think I'm pregnant."

"Oh," I said, "that's awful," and it was; it was the worst thing in the world. She was a faithful Catholic from a fierce devout family, and there would be no solutions but plenty of guilt, lies and pain. "God," I said, "What're you going to do?"[7]

I cannot easily support my conviction that Skillings's story is graceful, moving, and full of art. The person who finds the lines I have quoted to be trite and vapid would, for the moment, have the better of the argument. I can say, however, that, having found the story to be as good as I say it is, and having invited a suspended judgment of the person who hears those lines, I would go on to take note of the most remarkable aspect of those lines. What is remarkable in that passage, a passage from a story that declares its sophistication in twenty different ways, is how little is done to that small, conventional situation, how little effort is expended to transform it into art, to render it as ironic vision, or to redeem it with the splendors of myth and symbol. If the scene can honestly be called banal, Skillings does absolutely nothing, at that point, to transcend that banality. It is as if certain writers of fiction, at the present time, were willing, at crucial moments, to assert, with an absence of irony and a minimum of craft, the truth of certain truisms.

I suggest some of these truisms. The pleasure of sex is so implicitly denied in so much fiction of the fifties and sixties that it becomes a kind of shock to recover and present the truism that sex is, indeed, fun. The fragmentation and inefficacy of the nuclear family is so implicitly insisted upon in so much fiction of the fifties and sixties that it becomes a kind of shock to recover and present the truism, that the

[7] *Antaeus* 13/14 (Spring/Summer 1974):316.

nuclear family is still there, altered perhaps, damaged perhaps, but still there, father still meaning well, mother still persevering, children still doing those archetypal things that children have done. And the incompetence of the professions is so implicitly insisted upon in so much fiction of the fifties and sixties that it becomes a kind of shock to recover and present the truism that doctors sometimes cure.

Obviously in the long run *Nickel Mountain, Beyond the Bedroom Wall,* and the story by Skillings must justify themselves and make their way in the world not by the voguishness of their sensibility but by the coherence of their vision and by the art of their prose. But short of that final evaluation, one does take note of the voguishness, which is to say one takes note of a different sensibility, which finds ways of reanimating sentimentality, cultivating vulnerability, and discovering a plain responsiveness to other people scarcely possible in serious fiction since the Victorians.

In a climate in which that old defensive posture is unattractive, the possible ways of imagining living in the world with a rich responsiveness to other people is infinite. John Hawkes, for example, seems unlikely to present such a responsiveness, with his customary affinity for the surreal and his apparent lack of interest in social texture. Yet *The Blood Oranges* imagines each of its four figures as being moved and delighted by the other three in ways no reader of earlier Hawkes could have anticipated. Brautigan, for all of his self-regarding preciosity, still knows how to make a world in which the interest resides in its human variety. And, in what is the most extraordinary example of all, Stanley Elkin invests a perfectly amazing energy in a gallery of figures—a landlord, a disk jockey, a bailsman, an owner and manipulator of franchises, a liquor store owner—that most novelists of the earlier period would have written off

as vulgar figures of the commercial world, easily carica-
tured, devoid of mind, taste, and human integrity.

Why that older mode generated the self-imitating power
it did has something to do with the potency of the conventions governing the first-person narrators who generally focus such books, wily, ironic, and narcissistic, and it has
something to do with the shared belief in a stark and simple
adversary relationship between self and world. As a measure of how much we have changed, I quote the gentle,
understated dedication of Grace Paley's *Enormous Changes
at the Last Minute*, a dedication useful to my purpose not
only because of the sensibility it represents but also because of its reminder of the glib scorn that fifties novels so
easily found in the images of failed doctor and failed father.
"Everyone in this book," she writes, "is imagined into life
except the father. No matter what story he has to live in,
he's my father. I. Goodside, M.D., artist, and storyteller."

CHAPTER FIVE

Sentimentality, Old and New

HAVING POINTED TO CERTAIN WORKS AND CERTAIN TEN-
DENCIES in recent fiction and the general sensibility that I
have called tender or vulnerable, I have gone on, in the
last chapter, to use the word *sentimental*, a calculated risk,
because it is still, no matter how we have changed, the
single pejorative word from our shared critical vocabulary
that most easily damns. Of a work that may well be graceful
and articulate in its prose, its form full of energy and insight, if it seems properly called sentimental, we tend to
feel nothing more need be said as we watch the work re-
cede into oblivion. A single word with such power is in-
sidious: life and art are more complicated and more fluid
than the ritual use of the word will allow. Those quintessential experiences of high sentimentality are, of course,
unrecoverable for us. We will not again gather on the docks
to wait for the uncrating of the volumes of *The Old Curiosity Shop* to learn if Little Nell has died. But the extraordinary valuation we once placed upon detachment and
control are unrecoverable as well. We will not again find
an easy and automatic approval in the amazing submer-
gence of Eliot's personal anguish in the dry, austere,

mythic intricacies of his poetry. One does wish the word *sentimental* wasn't there, but it is. Lacking a more refined critical vocabulary, one's most responsible act, perhaps, is to find out how the word happens to mean as it does and how, with some adjustments, it can come to name qualities in recent fiction that are not necessarily soft-minded, not necessarily ephemeral, and not necessarily aesthetically irresponsible.

I have posed some examples in the last chapter that will serve as preliminary exhibits for this one. I add two more.

The literature of heavy sentimentality is characterized not only by a tone and a vision of experience but by certain characteristic events and certain rhetorical tactics. Mrs. Wood's *East Lynne*, for example, concludes an early chapter in this way: "And, with the hundred pounds in his pocket and desolation at his heart, the ill-fated young man once more quitted his childhood's home. Mrs. Hare and Barbara watched him steal down the path in the tell-tale moonlight, and gain the road, both feeling that those farewell kisses they had pressed upon his lips would not be renewed for years, and might be never." It is hardly necessary to lay out the context of those two sentences, to analyze the event and the diction with which it is rendered, to understand that, with such a passage, we are in the presence of a sentimental book.

Considered, for a moment, only from such a point of view, an atomistic sense of its characteristic events and rhetorical tactics, I suggest, first, the example of Spencer Holst's short fiction.[1] It contains an interest in distressed families, orphans, and frustrated lovers (an immigrant family that inadvertently throws away a bag containing thirty-eight thousand dollars with the garbage); a will to recover the pain of childhood ("If you've never swallowed

[1] *Spencer Holst Stories* (New York: Horizon, 1976).

a gumball you won't know what I mean."); an uncommon affection for animals (a character who develops what is virtually a marital love for a parrot); an unusual interest in those who, working within a stylized profession, work at that profession with extraordinary eccentricity (a baseball player who confounds the opposing team by bunting with the bat held vertically, so that the bat shoots "straight up twenty feet into the air" while the ball "would shoot straight down to the ground, landing an inch or two in front of home plate"); a tendency to self-deprecation ("Once upon a time there was a man who was. . . . It's hard to explain."); a fondness for the miniature (a bonsai mangrove swamp, complete with almost-invisible flying insects); a sensitivity to the difficulties of moving among cultures (an Appalachian in Scotland who, in attempting to make moonshine, invents Scotch); death and amazing survival (a small group of people who survive a hurricane tidal wave); and a fondness for the fragmentary. The following fiction I quote in its entirety: "He built his house over the elevator shaft of an abandoned salt mine, and in his house there was a small room whose only window was a trap door in the floor. He was a collector of cymbals, and whenever he got hold of a cymbal he would drop it down the shaft, and listen to it echo as it fell. He was a writer like me."

Lest Holtst's fiction, which is not widely known, should seem marginal whimsy, I cite the tributes to his work from the dust jacket, where his art is praised by Allen Ginsberg, Muriel Rukeyser, W. S. Merwin, John Hollander, Diane Wakoski, and John Cage. That his work is sentimental may be less than self-evident; but then, as I have begun to suggest, the word is far from precise. That his work should seem, in any case, to be open to odd moments of compassion, at once traditional and contemporary, is surely clear.

Secondly, I suggest John Irving's *The World According to Garp*. Highly praised yet open to the criticism that it is all things to all people, it is, in some sense, just that: stylized and naturalistic, grotesque and familiar, flip and thoughtful, facile and engaged, knowing and innocent, cynical and naïve. Irving's book, above all, is distant and detached when that seems a good idea to Irving or tender and open to feeling when that seems inevitable. Garp dreams that one of his sons, traveling in an airplane with his father, has tried to find the bathroom, alone, confused. Garp is irritated at his inability to find his own way; the child meanwhile has opened the wrong door and been sucked into space. Horrified at the disappearance of his son, Garp demands to know where the door leads, opens it himself, and follows his son to the ground. Nothing in the passage solicits a tear—it is, after all, a dream—and nothing in its rhetoric addresses our built-in vulnerability to moments of domestic pathos. It is briskly narrated, with no adjectival special effects, no lingering glances, no parting words. Yet the dream passage is enormously affecting, carrying in its two pages a sense of the pathos of father-and-son relationships and a sense, which increases as the book progresses, of the doom that underlies our dailiness. Sentimental seems far less applicable to Irving's passage than it does to the fiction of Holst. Yet the dream passage is one no modernist would have written and an area of experience no modernist would have tapped, and it bears a certain kinship with those passages from the fiction of the past we would easily call sentimental. Our awkwardness not only in naming such a quality but in placing it within a responsible discursive framework implies what I have promised, the need to discover how that heavily operative word means.

In trying to define *sentimentality*, it has been customary to locate our sense of the term in one of five areas. We say, first, that sentimentality is the result of the author's wish to play upon our emotions, by which we ordinarily mean his

wish to play strongly and directly upon our responsiveness
to pathos and our readiness to sympathize with misfortune.
Such a definition locates the idea in the intention of the
author, seeing the author either as a sentimental person
himself, deliberately wishing to pass on to his readers his
own mawkish view of life, or an unsentimental person,
cynically manipulating his readers. Most critics are not so
punctilious about violating the intentional fallacy as critics
once were. And there are certainly ways in which one can
speak of intentions, at least implicit intentions, with some
responsibility. Still, using a concept rooted in imputed intentions for the purpose of making qualitative judgments is
a risky business. Condemning an author because of his intention to manipulate the reader hardly clarifies the idea.
All writers wish to manipulate the reader; that is what the
rhetoric of fiction is all about. Sterne and Dickens manipulate resolutely and even obsessively, with what seems to be
a very rich and sensitive consciousness of what they are
doing. And the idea of separating writers with a mawkish
view of life from those without seems to me arrogant and
supercilious. Richardson probably had a mawkish view of
life, if that phrase means anything. But he wrote a great
book. The Victorians especially—Ruskin and Morris are
good examples—seem to have been very good at holding
in their minds ideas and impulses both soft and hard, open
and defensive, ironic and tender. There is, in short, no way
into the intention of the writer that can survive a moment's
scrutiny if we use that view of his intention as a way of
separating good from bad, true from false, superficial from
dense. Who, finally, knows or cares what an author wished
to do; and what kind of arrogance permits us to derogate
his work on the basis, mainly, of our reading of his imputed
motives?

The reverse of an intentional definition is an affective
one that locates sentimentality in our response. There are

probably instances in which an affective definition has been stated with detachment and rigor. But the common references of any such definition, expressed or implied, are obviously to weeping, or wishing to weep, the constrictions of the throat, the pathetic sigh, in the iconography of the eighteenth century the single tear; in short, those emotional responses that are felt in the very musculature of the body itself. The problems in working out an affective definition to anything, however, are enormous. I can recall an old teacher who wept, semester after semester, at the end of *Beowulf*. And if a reader were to weep at the end of a work that we ordinarily regard as being tough and ironic, *A Handful of Dust*, say, or *A Farewell to Arms*, who is to say he is behaving inappropriately? It seems to me likely that an affective definition of sentimentality originates not with any clear sense of the legitimate limits of a work's emotive power but with a vague uneasiness about the act of crying or being touched in analogous ways over a book, which is felt to be in and of itself an improper thing to do.

Another way of understanding sentimentality is to derive the concept from implicit standards of artistic proportion. Sentimentality, in this sense, is an expression of emotion in excess of the occasion. Again it need hardly be said that such a definition begs all questions. Rabelais's sensuality is excessive; Smollett's brutality is excessive; Sterne's verbality is excessive. The landscape of Emily Brontë and Hardy, the characters of Dickens and Thackeray, the style of Meredith and James all are done excessively. And in listing the excesses of *Finnegans Wake*, one hardly knows where to begin. Literature is always excessive, judged from the perspective of good taste and sensible proportion. Try taking any fictional event and, thinking of it as a bare event, decide how much emotion is appropriate to it: the discovery of Square in Molly Seagrim's bedroom, the birth of Frankenstein's creature, the death of Casaubon, Leopold Bloom eating breakfast. To define sentimentality as emotion in excess of the occasion is to lay oneself under the obligation of defining, before and after the fact, what degree of emotional expression is suitable to any occasion. A more hazardous critical enterprise is difficult to imagine.

Sentimentality has sometimes been described by reference to a peculiar, presumably failed, set of stylistic traits. Everyone recognizes how an author's stylistic vehicle may serve him in different ways. It may seem original, careful, evocative when he is dealing with journeys and meetings, dinner parties, and grand balls. But when he turns to partings and broken friendships, death and dying, his vehicle seems to fail him and he seems to lapse into a diction that is highly conventional, apparently a pastiche of archaic phrases, stylized figures, and formulaic devices. Why such a shift toward greater conventionality of style should take place when an author deals with certain subjects seems to me an interesting and utterly unexplored question. We have long since come to terms with highly conventionalized, highly stylized works in other genres, such as the Petrarchan sonnet sequence, whose power derives to a large extent from their ability to invest a small measure of individuality in a form and a body of images that are very much "received." But we seem incapable of dealing intelligently with imitative forms in prose fiction, and one of the more damning things we can say about a novelist is that he is imitative. In any case, locating our sense of what sentimentality means in the presence or absence of what we permit ourselves to call clichés is plainly unsatisfactory. Great prose often tends toward the imitative, the conventional, and the formulaic when it touches very basic subjects: the liturgy of Cranmer, *Pilgrim's Progress*, the prayers of Samuel Johnson, the most public essays of the Victorian sages, the wartime addresses of Churchill, almost anybody's most deeply felt letters. What we need to do is to accommodate ourselves to the possibility that fiction, like literature of any other genre, may move, even within the same work, between modes more conventional and less conventional and that such a rhythm does not, in itself, vitiate the work.

Finally it is possible to define and describe sentimentality by reference to artistic truth. Sentimentality, seen in this way, is that quality of literature in which the author takes one of the most crucial and sensitive of areas, the representation and evocation of the pathetic emotions, and simplifies his conflicts, turns his moral agents into crude types, and cuts off any possibility of reflection, especially as that reflection would turn itself toward the ambiguity and contradictoriness of experience. Sentimentality, according to such a view, is, in short, a lie. There is much to be said for using the word in that way: it has a kind of directness and courage about it that makes the other definitions seem evasive by comparison. But the problems with such an approach are considerable, all the same.

To speak of an artistic lie is, of course, to put oneself under the obligation of defining artistic truth. No one would hesitate to attempt to define artistic truth as that truth which is manifest in Chaucer's general prologue or the opening scene of *King Lear*. But let us imagine a definition of truth that we can work with in considering the varieties of prose fiction, a definition that would apply with equal pertinence to Gissing, James, Wells, Firbank, A. A. Milne, late Conrad, and Baron Corvo. The only definition of artistic truth that would serve such various writers would be one that is platitudinous and truistic. Most of us do, in fact, use an approach to artistic truth that is flexible, eclectic, and *ad hoc*, moreover one that allows for large variations in specificity of surface or stylization, large variations in moral ambiguity or moral clarity, large variations in the presentation of the emotions.

It does seem to me that those passages and works that have been judged sentimental ought to be subject to our continuing judgments regarding their artistic truth and that such judgments are both necessary and extremely difficult because of the mixed attraction and repulsion that such a mode may have for us. But it also seems to me that a plain equating of sentimentality and mendacity obscures more than it clarifies. It implies that artistic truth lies only within those areas that are ironic, tough, Apollonian, guarded, understated. Both Scott and Jane Austen realized that one can have both a Scott and a Jane Austen. The tribulations of Jeanie Deans may never again move readers in the way that the moral education of Emma Woodhouse interests us. But that is not to say that the tribulations of Jeanie Deans are all a lie.

We have reasoned badly. Why we have reasoned as badly as we have is obvious. We have sought to rationalize a critical response to literature on the basis of a limited sense of appropriate responses fashionable for seventy-five years but by no means universal, culturally or historically. What we can now do as human beings is to admit what we already knew: Leslie Fiedler, not long ago, would integrate into his public lectures an image of himself sitting in a warm bath, reading *Little Dorrit*, the tears running down his cheeks, mingling with the bath water. What we can do as readers and critics is to work toward a more lively awareness of the possibilities contained within the sentimental mode and a greater flexibility in the way in which we use the term.

We can remind ourselves, for example, of the enormous number of ways in which a writer who occupies the sentimental mode, who commits himself to the accessibility of the emotions, and who exploits all of the rhetorical devices appropriate to that mode can still acknowledge the contradictoriness and the irony of experience. The jazz lyric makes a useful analogy. The lyrics of most popular songs are vacuous and simple-minded, sentimental in the most pejorative sense. But sung by Jelly Roll Morton or Billie Holiday, they take on a set of embellishments that pay constant tribute to the ironic view of experience, all without qualifying the basic commitment to the sentimental view of experience that the words of the song, by themselves, communicate.

All literature of permanent value contains compassion and reserve, openness and defensiveness in some proportion: Swift's *Modest Proposal* is a devastating exercise in irony—and an overwhelmingly compassionate work. A view of literature that overvalues irony is in danger of attending too little to the compassion in ironic works. Conversely, a view of literature that deprecates sentimentality is in danger of attending too little to the richness of texture, indeed the wholeness of vision, which unabashedly sentimental works can contain. Certainly, a taste among writers of quality for only the reserved and ironic runs the risk, when the pendulum has swung, of seeming remote and overintellectualized, distant and cold. The pendulum, as I have suggested, has swung.

There is a moment in Vonnegut's *Slaughterhouse-Five* in which the awful nihilism that the experience of the book induces together with the arch, self-regarding preciosity with which the book is conceived all come together. Remarkably Sternean, the moment is also remarkably sentimental, in that nonpejorative sense I have tried to allow for. Billy Pilgrim has been captured by the Germans, taken to a prison camp where, frightened and exhausted, he is, at last, fed well. In the night, he approaches the latrine, from which he can hear the sounds of wailing.

Billy looked inside the latrine. The wailing was coming from in there. The place was crammed with Americans who

had taken their pants down. The welcome feast had made
them as sick as volcanoes. The buckets were full or had
been kicked over.

An American near Billy wailed that he had excreted
everything but his brains. Moments later he said, "There
they go, there they go." He meant his brains.

That was I. That was me. That was the author of this
book.[2]

Sentimentality, in its classic forms, is antithetical to
irony. Irony, from a position of some detachment, regards
the objects of its contemplation with an unresolved doubleness. Don Quixote is both certifiably mad and transcen-
dently heroic. In *Death in Venice*, the claims of the flesh
are both coarse, repellent, perverse *and* credible, touching, altogether human. Sentimentality, on the other hand,
makes discrete distinctions and assigns unambivalent values. There is no doubleness about stray dogs, orphans at
Christmas, and lovers irrevocably separated.

In the passage from Vonnegut, however, one has, curiously, both sentimentality and irony. The illusion of the
novel collapses for a moment and one is invited to feel
enormous compassion both for Billy Pilgrim, within the
novel, and Kurt Vonnegut, Jr., in the world, both of them
victims of the fire-bombing of Dresden and the politics of
death, both of them frightened, tired, cold, and alone. Si-
multaneously one is invited to enter into an ironic contemplation of the world in which the grotesque has become
domesticated and the absurd has become lovable. It is as if
Camus's Sisyphus, that quintessential absurdist figure,
rolling his awesome rock up his austere mountain, only to
have it roll, inexorably, down again, were presented to us
as a waif, with knickers and an unruly forelock, implicitly
soliciting tenderness and the luxury of a single tear.

It is an unpretentious passage, in Vonnegut's novel, yet

[2] *Slaughterhouse-Five* (New York: Dell, 1971), p. 125.

it accomplishes a minor miracle of the creative imagination. It manages, somehow, to merge the ironic with the
sentimental, to domesticate the absurd, so that the reader
is forced into both a detached contemplation of the doubleness of the scene, the excremental ridiculousness of it all
coexisting with a horror of the particular bestiality of that
episode of the war *and* a profound compassion for the vulnerability of the two lost little boys who lie at the center of
the scene.

Or consider a passage from Robert Pirsig's *Zen and the
Art of Motor-Cycle Maintenance*:

> I suppose if I were a novelist rather than a Chautauqua
> orator I'd try to "develop the characters" of John and Sylvia
> and Chris with action-packed scenes that would also reveal
> "inner meanings" of Zen and maybe Art and maybe even
> Motorcycle Maintenance. That would be quite a novel, but
> for some reason I don't feel quite up to it. They're friends,
> not characters, and as Sylvia herself once said, "I don't like
> being an object!" So a lot of things we know about one an-
> other I'm simply not going into. Nothing bad, but not really
> relevant to the Chautauqua. That's the way it should be
> with friends.[3]

As with the passage from Vonnegut, the illusion of Pirsig's
novel, if it is a novel, breaks down and the novelist, as
novelist, enters, characteristically with stylistic overtones
of willed naïveté, self-denigration, and a diction that looks
both ways—to a wily management of narrative presentation and to a low-colloquial elevation of authenticity over
craft. At that moment, he allows to coexist a genuine tenderness for the companions of his journey, friends for
whom their mutual bond transcends his ability to write
about it, along with a certain detachment and doubleness,
their homely friendship existing in a book that is ultimately

[3](New York: Morrow, 1974), pp. 137–38.

about madness and the will to live, quality and cultural debasement.

Or consider a passage from a talent now somewhat faded but still symptomatic, Richard Brautigan.

> "It was light and halfway through the dawn. Foster was busy sweating away in his T-shirt, even though we found the morning to be a little chilly. During the years that I had known Foster, I'd never seen him when he wasn't sweating. It was probably brought about by the size of his heart. I was always certain that his heart was as big as a canteloupe and sometimes I went to sleep thinking about the size of Foster's heart."[4]

For a passage that obviously strives for an offhand, artless effect, it is, in fact, highly contrived, with its manipulation of the literal and metaphorical sense of Foster's large heart. Still, the illusion of amateurishness remains, an amateurishness that suggests similarities with the authorial attitudes of the other two examples. Like those other examples, the speaker of the passage permits a sensitivity to people, in the shape of simple verbal gestures of affection, to threaten the very order and control of the fiction.

Sentimentality is rarely indiscriminate. Even those writers who seem deeply and thoroughly sentimental still select the objects of their feelings in highly patterned and predictable ways, according to fashion, convention, and their own predispositions. A tenderness toward place is by no means constant in sentimental literature, nor is a tenderness toward physical objects; rather both follow certain fluctuations of taste. And although a special tenderness toward people is essential to sentimentality, the nature of the people responded to and the modes of presentation vary, in the same way, according to convention and taste. Inevitably, a pattern emerges from the examples I have cited, in

[4] *The Abortion: An Historical Romance* (New York: Pocket Books, 1972), p. 102.

which the writers, all legatees of Sterne, contrive their most tender effects so as to coincide with their moments of technical reflexiveness and self-irony, allowing their tenderness toward other people to become, at the same time, tenderness toward themselves. The humbleness and fragility of the characters who are the objects of the tenderness are made to coincide with the humbleness and fragility of the author. And the air of the grotesque or eccentric or absurd that hovers over each of the three passages is made to seem familiar, deserving of compassion and affection.

I suggest a further range of exhibits: A well-received first novel by Thomas McMahon called *Principles of American Nuclear Chemistry: A Novel*, remarkably tender and unabashedly sentimental. The evocation of place in Updike, especially the places of youth. Another first novel, by Gilbert Sorrentino, called *Steelwork*, technically a narrative collage, yet charged with a nostalgic fondness for the places and people of the author's youth. The two brilliant novels of Larry Woiwode, *What I'm Going to Do, I Think* and *Beyond the Bedroom Wall*, both of them lyrical, deeply felt, sentimental. Certain passages in the fiction of Peter Beagle. Certain passages in the fiction of Robley Wilson, Jr. Certain passages in the fiction of Russell Banks. Certain passages in the fiction of William Kotzwinkle. The recent fiction of Harold Brodkey, which manages not only to be both ironic and sentimental but also pornographic and tender. A novelistic autobiography, or an autobiographical novel, called *Stop-Time*, by Frank Conroy, lyrical and evocative in its prose, eccentric and neurotic in its human images, deeply feeling in its emotional posture, from which I quote some chapter titles: "Hate, and a Kind of Music," "Please Don't Take My Sunshine Away," "The Coldness of Public Places," "Hanging On," "Losing My Cherry," "Going to Sea," "Elsinore, 1953." John Gardner's *Grendel*.

Of course fiction now is no more monolithic than it has ever been. And there are figures who escape the tendency I describe, some of them major figures. Among writers whose techniques are basically realistic, Bellow is an obvious exception, a writer of extraordinary power and depth of feeling who has never written a passage that would seem to justify, even in a nonpejorative sense, the word *sentimental*. Among postrealistic writers, Pynchon is the most obvious case of a major talent for whom the sentimental is uncongenial. Of course it is a tendency that I describe. And that tendency implies that when an absurdist aesthetic has gone as far as it can, in late Beckett, say, or in some of Barth (or in silence), it has become, for all of its integrity of motive and consistency of execution, to certain writers, not all, a lie to experience.

No one now writes fiction well without basing his view of the world on his own version of that sense of the nature of things we have come to call—by an extension of Camus— the absurd. But a substantial number of writers have, by some miracle of the imagination, salvaged from the wreckage a legitimate capacity to feel with a revised version of an old-fashioned tenderness, to be touched with the classic pathos of vulnerability, and to drop their defenses—well, partly drop their defenses, since the fiction that results is mannered and self-conscious, artful and precise, and nobody believes, as he is reading it, that he has inadvertently picked up *East Lynne* or a Dickens death scene. What one does know is that the use of *sentimentality* as an automatic pejorative is no longer legitimate and that modes of feeling in the culture at large and in the art of fiction in particular now exist that would have been suppressed, denied, edited out, and argued away a generation ago.

CHAPTER SIX

Naïve Narration:
Classic to Postmodern

Cɪɒssɪc ʇo Poꙅʇɯoqǝɹɯ
Nɒïʌǝ Nɒɹɹɒʇɪoɯ:

ONE OF RUSSELL EDSON'S REMARKABLE FABLES reads like this, in its entirety:

The Clothes Closet

A clothes closet said to a woman, come. Which she did, into it. And it shut its door around her.

She said, I don't love you. The closet pressed her closer with its door.

I don't love you, she said.

Father's fedora fell against her cheek. She was pressed against father's great coat.

Oh please let me go, she cried.

She began to cry.[1]

I, for one, find the fable oddly affecting, yet the reader who found it trivial would not be responding in a way altogether surprising. An experienced reader can hardly be expected to carry with him a taste for fables, and this one, especially, seeks to cast itself into the voice of a particularly childlike

[1] *The Very Thing That Happens* (Norfolk, Conn: New Directions, 1964), p. 13.

intelligence. Mann and Joyce knew more than we do and
they manipulate their language with a resonance that an
infinite number of rereadings will not fully comprehend.
That is what modern fiction does, and it is consequently
unsettling to confront a childlike voice narrating a fiction
some sixty words long. Yet one reflects, first, on the way in
which we have learned to adapt ourselves to the child's eye
in the visual arts: the stick figures of Klee, for example.
One reflects on the way in which Edson's fable presents
domestic space, claustrophobic, attractive and fatal, full of
the union of father and clothes, without reflection, without
analysis, in a way that the classic modernists would have
neither wished nor been able to do. And one reflects on
the kinship of Edson's naïve narration with the sentimental
mode for which I have tried to establish a legitimacy. And
one concludes that there may well be an aesthetic authority
in what Edson does that a first reading may not suggest.

If the child-mind of Edson's narrator is startling in its
departure from the dense and knowing modes of modernism, it is less startling in the context of historical possibilities. As always, it is useful to back up and see where we
have come, because the possibilities of naïve narration are
very old and very rich. One place to begin is with the six-
teenth-century picaresque novel *Lazarillo de Tormes*.

Lazarillo has suffered all the abuse he can endure from
his first master, who is blind. In order to proceed further,
he tells his master they must first jump a large ditch. The
blind man asks Lazarillo to lead him to the narrowest part
of the ditch so that he can jump it. Lazarillo leads him to a
position directly in front of a stone pillar; the master takes
a running leap, crashes into it, and falls to the ground "half
dead with his head split open." "I left him," says Lazarillo
in the Donald Frame translation, "in the care of a crowd of
people who came out to help him and set off running to the
town gates; before nightfall I was in Torrijos. I never found

out what happened to him and I did not bother to inquire either."

As a whole, *Lazarillo de Tormes* exhibits control, conscious artifice, and irony.[2] But at that moment, and elsewhere, the anonymous author does not merely affect the voice suggestive of a hungry and clever boy but writes, ventriloquist style, as if the words issued from the boy himself. Lazarillo does not know what happened to the master because he has hit the road for Torrijos. What's more, he doesn't care. When Lazarillo doesn't know something that he thinks we might be curious about, he tells us he doesn't know. And when he simplifies or omits, we understand it as the plausible utterance of a child-mind. Not having learned the rituals of awe, reverence, and circumlocution, the narrating picaro can see the official superstructure of his society for what it is, largely a hollow and self-important organization of pious frauds dedicated to the perpetuation of their own power. Not having learned how to intellectualize, however, he does not tell us how fraudulent the upper-dogs of his society are, seeing his world in narrow terms of hunger, pain, humiliation, revenge, and survival, leaving us to draw the general conclusions, which are more potent because they have been only implied. Such are the standard advantages of naïve narration, by which I mean narration that seems to issue from a mind simpler, more vulnerable, more direct in the forms of its expression, more given to the visual than to the intellectual, less given to subtlety and fine discrimination, more free of ritual inhibition and social constraint than the implied audience for which a book seems to be written.[3]

[2] By using Lazarillo as an example of naïve narration, I do not mean to minimize either the art of the book or the problematic nature of its narration. Both are superbly treated in Stephen Gilman's "The Death of Lazarillo de Tormes," *PMLA* 81 (1966):149–66.

[3] I have used the word *naïve* as my operative epithet, deliberately avoiding the word *innocent* whenever possible. Partly because of the Blakean

We may make several judgments as a result of Lazaro's simplicity, but all of our judgments move in a similar direction, toward filling the gaps, providing the complexity, adding the feeling tone to passages that seem insufficiently felt, assenting to the plain truths that the picaro's naïveté reveals, in general making mature sense out of a boy's story. Naïveté may be put to purposes that are not necessarily aesthetically superior to the purposes of *Lazarillo* but that exploit several levels and call upon a number of responses. "Nothing could be so beautiful, so smart, so brilliant, so well drilled," writes Voltaire in *Candide*,

> as the two armies. Trumpets, fifes, oboes, drums, cannons formed a harmony such as was never heard even in hell. First the cannons felled about six thousand men on each side; then the musketry removed from the best of worlds some nine or ten thousand scoundrels who infected its surface. The bayonet also was the sufficient reason for the death of some thousands of men. The whole might well amount to about thirty thousand souls. Candide, trembling like a philosopher, hid himself as best he could during this heroic butchery. Finally, while both kings were having *Te Deums* sung, each in his own camp, he decided to go reason elsewhere about effects and causes.

Consider first the kinds of simplicity represented. *Naïve* is not the right word for men shown en masse, but they are represented as automata, supremely stupid, marching off to their own slaughter with an excess of military zeal and a

---

power the word still carries, *innocence* is widely used by writers on fiction; although it overlaps the concept I am describing, it is not identical with it. Nearly all novels render a transition from innocence to experience, but that innocence may be anything but naïve. Most American characters in Henry James's novels, for example, are innocent at the beginning of the novels and often at the end. But that innocence, a spontaneity and lack of guile rather than a simplicity and immaturity, is generally an aspect of a personality that is subtle and sophisticated in innumerable other ways. Naïveté of narration is something else again, a special mode of telling that James, to return to the example, never uses, despite his fascination with the forms of innocence.

poverty of brain. The kings are represented as hypocritical fools, players with lives by the thousand. Candide is represented as being extraordinarily naïve, not in the sense, like Lazarillo, of being boyish and limited in his judgments, rather as being overequipped with philosophical jargon and underequipped with common sense. The narrator himself, of course, is naïve: the way to Voltaire's irony is for him to tell his story in a way so morally callous, stylistically inept, and simple-minded as to stagger the imagination. As we read, we respond variously to the kings, who are naïve and have power, to the soldiers, who are naïve and do not, and to Candide, who is eager and attractive but supremely obtuse.

But what is most central to *Candide* is the double way in which we must read the narration, admiring the art but correcting the judgments, knowing that the controlling, creating intelligence behind the work is one of the finest minds of the Enlightenment, obliged to respond to the Panglossian formulae and the facile militaristic trumpery that are, in that passage, his primary rhetorical devices. Naïveté in *Lazarillo* gives to the picaro a clarity of vision against the corruption of the world. Nothing could be further from the purposes of *Candide*. Naïveté in *Candide* never reveals a superior truth to the mind open to the pathos, corruption, and injustice of the world. Naïveté in Candide obliges us to correct it in a dozen different ways, with superior knowledge, with an acute sense of precision in language and a distaste for professional jargon, with moral outrage, with compassion for suffering, and always with a quest for the author, who never quite reveals himself without tongue in cheek and mock naïveté on his face.

Sterne, more than anyone else in the eighteenth and nineteenth centuries, presents different possibilities of naïve narration. Readers of *Tristram Shandy* and *Sentimental Journey* will recall how both the characters and the narrator are vulnerable to contingency; digressive, easily diverted, tender, easily moved by suffering and pathos, sentimental; comic, eccentric, easily caught off guard; irresolute, full of purpose but given to failure; uncertain of their field of vision, panoramic, encyclopedic at one moment, minute and microscopic the next; sensual and flirtatious, failed and impotent; verbal, voluble, a veritable library of words; and troubled, involuted, halting, and inarticulate. Sterne's two major works seem to be perfect fusions of world view and manner, and no reader of these novels is surprised to find that the Reverend Sterne was digressive, anecdotal, foolish, indecorous, indiscreet, variously tender and insensitive, bawdy, impotent, self-mocking. By now a whole shelf of commentary exists to gloss Sterne's manner, which is to say it exists to gloss Sterne's naïveté, which can be summed up as the quintessential mannerisms of a sentimental age or the ironic mannerisms of a tough mind in a sentimental age, the mock fallibility of an extraordinary artist or the remarkable charting of the aleatory, nonlinear way that modern art would one day go. However one distributes one's emphases, the common reader is obliged to agree that the naïveté is both a function of the identity of the teller of Sterne's books and a function of the critique that Sterne creates of the very nature of telling itself. For to be naïve, for Sterne, is not only to open oneself before the indeterminacy of the world but it is also to declare one's reservations about the ability of words on a page to contain and convey significant experience.

In some sense, most of the novels of the eighteenth and nineteenth centuries contain versions of naïve narration. A number of novelists, for example, play here and there at self-derogation: Fielding, Thackeray, Trollope, Dickens, Meredith. Other novelists contrast forms of rustic simplicity with urban corruption, as Mrs. Gaskill does, or Hardy,

a contrast that lends itself to passages in which the novelist's voice is apt to take on a certain sympathetic naïveté.
Or novelists may exploit the comic resources latent in
naïve dialect, as a hundred American novelists do from
Twain to Ring Lardner. And the projection by the novelist
of a younger self as narrator and central character is a frequent nineteenth-century mode, as in early Dickens and
early Melville. It is the nature of the novel to maintain
reservations about fixed systems, to be skeptical about
power, to distrust abstract words, to regard ironically the
apparent wisdom of the mature, to convey discontent with
the institutional structure of the world, which is to say that
it is in the very nature of the novel to find uses for naïveté,
both in the telling and in the contained action. Yet sustained naïve narration is rare in the nineteenth century in
the sense of narration that consistently calls attention to
the fact that it is the telling of a mind demonstrably simpler
and less experienced than the ostensible mind of the author.

The great works of the modernist period contain within
them certain possibilities of naïve narration—Lawrence's
fiction is one example, Faulkner's another—but naïveté, as
a mode of narration, is not congenial to the great writers of
the modernist period. Hemingway's celebrated simplicity
of narration, for example, is not a function of naïveté. Density of reference, intricacy of construction, symbolic resonance, ironic poise, power of vision, phrases like these
come of mind to describe the manner of telling characteristic of Mann, Proust, Joyce, Woolf, any of the dominant
modernists. So it is with the end of modernism in our time.
The narrator of Beckett's *The Unnamable* may be inept and
impotent in a dozen different ways but he is not naïve. It
is, in fact, difficult to think of a serious work of fiction from
the end of the nineteenth century to the end of the Second
World War that contrives a story told more simply, with

less maturity and intricacy of judgment, less density of observation, less *mind* than the author presumably possesses himself and than he is willing to grant to his intended audience.

The American fifties is a different situation, for reasons that seem to be rooted in that bland and innocent time. The emblematic work for that period is surely Salinger's *Catcher in the the Rye*, a novel tarnished by the intervening years (I pull my Signet edition from the shelf to find the pages yellow and brittle) but still striking in the coherence of the voice it projects, a voice so memorable that features of it remain firmly lodged in the minds of most readers who have not reread it in those twenty-some years. Looking back at it now, that extraordinarily compelling naïveté of narration seems to be a result of several forces: a set of stylistic tics and ritual speech patterns ("That's something else that gives me a royal pain. I mean if you're good at writing compositions and somebody starts talking about commas."); an eccentric sense of detail that glosses and generalizes what an older speaker might make specific ("After I got all packed, I sort of counted my dough. I don't remember exactly how much I had, but I was pretty loaded."); a counter tendency toward an often startling freshness of perception, even a gratuitous specificity ("The blond I'd been dancing with's name was Bernice something—Crabs or Krebs. The two ugly ones' names were Marty and Laverne. I told them my name was Jim Steele, just for the hell of it."); a peculiar syntactic patterning, heavy on coordination, in which subordinate patterns, if they exist at all, exist as afterthoughts ("She said their house was right on the beach, and they had a tennis court and all, but I just thanked her and told her I was going to South America with my grandmother. Which was really a hot one, because my grandmother hardly even goes out of the *house*, except maybe to go to a goddam matinée or something."); and finally that insistent barrage of judgments, by means of which the moronic, the ugly, the crumby, the depressing, the not too hot, the boring, the flitty-looking, the very stupid, the dopey, the Yale-looking, the snobbish, the fat-assed, the dirty, the strange, the show-offy, the disgusting, the mean, the conceited, the phony, and, to be sure, the nice are tagged and discriminated.

It is not now and never was the kind of book that strikes readers as being a technical innovation, a judgment we usually grant to those fictions that do unusual things with structure rather than texture. Yet Salinger's novel constructs a naïve narration, with an ear for the spoken language, that is indisputably a tour de force, in the service of none of the classic purposes I have named, not for the satiric leverage possible when a naïve speaker views the corruption of the world, not for a demonstration of the perils and follies of a mechanistic response to the pain and uncertainty of the world, not for a dramatized rendering of the difficulty of living, extending to the very difficulty of getting one's story told. What Salinger's naïve narration exists for is something so plain and homely as what we used to call the creation of character; no bald statement of pragmatic design upon the reader can be adduced from his choice of a mode of narration simpler than the author's own ostensible voice. What is audacious is the totality of self-enclosure with which the book comes to us, a remarkably pure version of what Ihab Hassan has called radical innocence[4]—Holden's view unmodified by any other.

The whole of Hassan's book, as his title indicates, is involved with forms of innocence in the fiction of the fifties, with victims, schlemiehls, and ingénues faced with the rites either of suffering or initiation, against a background

[4]*Radical Innocence: Studies in the Contemporary American Novel* (Princeton: Princeton University Press, 1961).

of the leaden institutions of the world. Yet not one of the novelists Hassan discusses—Styron, Swados, Mailer, Buechner, Malamud, Ellison, Gold, Cheever, Donleavy, McCullers, Capote, or Bellow—uses a naïve narrator with anything like the sustained, *uncorrected* virtuosity of Salinger. Other novels show an innocence the writer understands and feels compassion for but does not share, addressed to an audience that can be expected to understand the innocence depicted without sharing it any more than the author does. Salinger's monologue, on the other hand, presents a totally inside view of the naïf—narrow, intransigent, and aesthetically limited, as Hassan says it is, and dreadfully time-bound, as we now know it to be. But for all that, Salinger's accomplishment suggests what every other novelist of the fifties wanted to do but couldn't, which was to present an inside view of naïveté.

I propose a transition to the postmodern imagination with a passage from Leonard Michaels.

> In the fifties I learned to drive a car. I was frequently in love. I had more friends than now.
> When Khrushchev denounced Stalin my roommate shit blood, turned yellow, and lost most of his hair.
> I attended the lectures of the excellent E. B. Burgum until Senator McCarthy ended his tenure. I imagined N.Y.U. would burn. Miserable students, drifting in the halls, looked at one another.
> In less than a month, working day and night, I wrote a bad novel.
> I went to school—N.Y.U., Michigan, Berkeley—much of the time.
> I had witty, giddy conversation, four or five nights a week, in a homosexual bar in Ann Arbor.
> I read literary reviews the way people suck candy.
> Personal relationships were more important to me than anything else.
> I had a fight with a powerful fat man who fell on my face and was immovable.

I had personal relationships with football players, jazz musicians, ass-bandits, nymphomaniacs, non-specialized degenerates, and numerous Jewish premedical students.

I had personal relationships with thirty-five rhesus monkeys in an experiment on monkey addiction to morphine. They knew me as one who shot reeking crap out of cages with a hose.[5]

Ordinarily, if a writer projects a younger self more-or-less identifiable with his mature self, he seeks some means of dramatizing the naïveté while maintaining the control and art that demonstrate his distance, as writer, from that naïveté. We need to know that the mature Dickens understands Pip, knows how he talks and feels, even is able to render aspects of his inner life, the child's-eye view of the physical world, for example. At the same time, we need to be perpetually reassured, by the style and art of the author, that the mature Dickens has distanced Pip, focused him in his imagination, and comprehended him. Such is the customary narrative situation of the *Bildungsroman*. We never doubt the art and maturity of Joyce and Lawrence while we are being presented with the innocence of Stephen Dedalus and Paul Morel.

Salinger breaks with that tradition, leaving us with the experiencing voice of the younger self and nothing of the mature self but the craft. Leonard Michaels goes a step farther, and it is difficult to think of anything remotely like it before the seventies. The author's narrating self does not superimpose a mature manner upon the remembered, experiencing self. Rather, the narrating self is, in its own way, just as naïve. Those flat, discontinuous sentences are oddly evocative of the process of remembering. But they do not evoke that earlier self with an added increment of wisdom and style, as the *Bildungsroman* always does. Maturity is

[5] *I Would Have Saved Them If I Could* (New York: Farrar, Straus & Giroux, 1975), pp. 59–60.

no longer a useful concept. The transition is not from innocence to experience but from innocence to innocence.

It is impossible to overestimate the effect of the nonsequential, discontinuous progress of Michaels's prose. We
easily accept a verbal collage when it seems to derive from
the visual world of immediate experience. Of course the
urban landscape is a collage. And a writer who works to
reproduce with words that visual effect is working out of an
ancient mimetic impulse. We easily accept a verbal collage
when it seems to derive not simply from photographic reality but from the bits and scraps that make up our consciousness of the world. Michel Butor's *Mobile*, with its
discontinuous segments of road maps, travel guides, radio
call letters, and Howard Johnson menus, seems less odd
now than it did when it appeared, because we have come
to understand how compellingly it represents the mind,
especially of a non-native, taking in the obsessive data of
the United States. Michaels's prose, however, makes a collage out of self-recollection, without cause or motive, without any of the psychological glue that holds together anybody else's recital of comparable events, without linearity
or necessary order. It is as reasonable to say of Michaels's
technique, as it is to say of Butor's, that the mind often
does work in that way. But the point is hardly to confirm
the legitimacy of Michaels by invoking psychology but
rather to point to the audacity of the experiment. There is
no body of fictive reminiscences before him that so star-
tlingly and compelling avoids *explaining*.

In more than its form Michaels's prose avoids explaining.
Naïveté in fictional narration is always highly rhetorical.
There is always a heightened sense of audience, a heightened sense of personal investment in the choice of words,
almost always indirection, feigning, irony. *Candide*, as I
suggest, seeks to work upon the reader relentlessly.
Sterne, in conveying his sense of the world, is compelled

to explain and explain—how he happens to be inept, how he can't get his story told, why he has the wrong name, all of this directed to "sir" and "madam." *Catcher in the Rye*, of course, is so relentlessly rhetorical that one comes away from it with the illusion of having experienced the book not through the eye, from a page, but through the ear, Holden Caulfield having selected us as one of the few non-phony people in the world, to whom he can explain, explain.

Leonard Michaels's prose, on the other hand, is not written *to* anybody. There is no implied audience. There is no set of common assumptions, no appeal to shared comic responses, no common morality. The prose seems to have no occasion; no one has asked Michaels what he did in the fifties. The words have no implied social setting. And the author does not seek to make friends with us, persuade us, involve us, tease us, or move us in any way. The prose may very well move us, to be sure, or at least strike us as being funny, and no doubt Michaels wishes to do this. But he does this without overt appeals and without any of the usual apparent tactics of the writer who seeks to use naïveté for a moral, political, even aesthetic purpose. That nonrhetorical naïveté is surprising when seen against the background of previous fiction; but it is a quality that Michaels shares with innumerable writers of the seventies.

Finally, Michaels's naïveté is not judgmental, either explicitly or implicitly. A judgmental quality in naïve narration is a function of the gap between the naïveté of characters and narrator on the one hand and the superior perspicacity of author and reader on the other. Voltaire's patent tongue in cheek turns Candide's naïveté into a commentary on the folly of the world. And even the absent Salinger sufficiently controls the judgmental activity of Holden so that we are compelled to assent, from time to time, with his complicity in Holden's exposure of fraudulence. Only Sterne, despite his obvious accumulation of vast erudition, still affects a posture no wiser as writer than he was as foetus and child. And in this respect Sterne and Michaels are comparable. Every human image in Michaels's fiction is fairly ridiculous, especially the image of the experiencing speaker. But nobody is judged as being morally deficient because Michaels, as narrator, will not permit himself that judicial distance.

It is easiest to describe Michaels's prose negatively, pointing to what it does not do, both against the background of previous naïve narration and the background of fictional possibilities in general. What it does do is this. First it achieves a remarkable clarity of outline, simplified and stylized to be sure, like panels in a cartoon series, but also sharp and memorable in a way that denser fiction of personal reminiscence now often fails to be. It finds an appropriate emotional response to the condition of having come of age in a shallow decade, a response that avoids the facile pleasure of nostalgia or the ease of self-pity, in favor of a spare, stark self-exposure. It contrives a narrative technique in which analysis, especially the sociopolitical claptrap that generally accompanies an evocation of the fifties, can be avoided, avoided obviously because it is distrusted. It revises the conventions by means of which the memory is represented on the page, rejecting the access to the consciousness claimed by the moderns—rich, dense, heavy with myth and symbol, full of sensibility, nuance, epiphany—in favor of a different artifice, no less persuasive, in which the memory operates rather like Kodachrome slides of an old vacation. Finally Michaels's prose represents the discovery of an appropriate form, namely the verbal collage that I earlier described, here an attempt to fix a personal vision of an age by cutting and pasting.

I suggest something of the range of naïve narration in the fiction of the last decade. Mitchell Sisskind begins his strange and wonderful story "A Mean Teacher" in this way:

There was no chalk in Miss Carter's room. It was gone. She wanted to write on the blackboard. I'll send a child to Miss Baylie's room, thought Miss Carter, to get some chalk. Still, she remembered: Miss Baylie is like an elephant. Who shall I send there, she wondered.

There were no troublemakers.

The children sat in blue desks, thinking: There is such a thing as ghosts. They read of other lands.[6]

Sisskind's story shares almost nothing with Michaels's technically or temperamentally. The one striking common characteristic is that both stories, coming from writers who surely could, had they chosen, have written "difficult," ironic, symbolic, modernist stories, are written naïvely.

Anything by Brautigan suggests further possibilities for naïve narration, as well as further risks, the possibilities lying in the exploitation of an openness and tenderness to experience rare in prose fiction, the risks being an arch, precious, cloying quality. The examples multiply. Robert Coover, plainly, is fascinated with the possibilities of naïve narration, as are, in their different ways, R. D. Skillings, Steve Katz, Russell Banks. And although the fiction of Barthelme does many things, one thing it certainly does is get told, ordinarily, by a voice simpler, plainer, more opaque and less intricate than the ostensible intelligence of Barthelme and Barthelme's readers.

Vonnegut's career is at once the most public and the most cultish of all the writers of postrealistic American fiction. But, despite the attention he has received, one feature of his work has gone largely unremarked. As Vonnegut has grown older, he has cultivated a style progressively more naïve so that now, in his fifties, he writes very like a child. Vonnegut has always found it useful to remind us that he comes from Indianapolis, where people talk like buzz saws

[6]*A Cinch: Amazing Works from the Columbia Review* (New York: Columbia University Press, 1969), p. 207.

and call themselves Hoosiers. An innocence both real and feigned has always been his ironic lever against the world. But *Breakfast of Champions* is far more pervasively naïve than anything else he has done. "Everybody in America was supposed to grab whatever he could and hold onto it. Some Americans were very good at grabbing and holding, were fabulously well-to-do. Others couldn't get their hands on doodley-squat."[7] Or elsewhere:

> Choo-choo trains and steamboats and factories had whistles which were blown by steam when Dwayne Hoover and Kilgore Trout and I were boys—when our fathers were boys, when our grandfathers were boys. The whistles looked like this: [Here Vonnegut inserts his own drawing of a steam whistle.]
>
> Steam from water boiled by burning coal was sent raging through the whistles, which made harshly beautiful laments, as though they were the voice boxes of mating or dying dinosaurs—cries such as *wooooooooo-uh*, *wooooo-uh*, and *Torrrrrrrrrrrrrrrrrrrrrrrrrrrnnnnnnnnnnnn*, and so on.[8]

As a measure of the distance of that passage from the great works of the modernist movement, I imagine trying to explain to Proust or Mann, Conrad or Henry James how it is possible that that was written by one of our more popular and highly regarded novelists.

No single formula will account for the varieties of naïve narration in the last decade. But beyond what I have said of Leonard Michaels's passage, it seems to me that the best generalizations build around the apparent tendency to find naïveté not inevitably funny (although it may be), not tactically useful (although it may be), but attractive in itself, as a way of being in the world. *Breakfast of Champions* is a grim and depressing book. The only thing that makes it

[7](New York: Delacorte Press, 1975), p. 13.
[8]Ibid., pp. 121–22.

tolerable is that sweet and stupid voice by means of which it gets told. Vulnerability is more attractive than defensiveness. A single-leveled style that has nothing to conceal is more attractive than the dense intellectuality that says more than it knows. Impulse is more attractive than prudence. Surprise is more attractive than already knowing. The writer of fiction has always been a god, making a world, devising fates, revealing minds. Nothing is more astonishing in the fiction of the present time than the writer's willingness not merely to diminish point of view— that has been done a thousand times—but to diminish his very appearance of knowing in pursuit of a human vision that he can bear to live with.

CHAPTER SEVEN

Mock-Fact
Ⅶ oⅽ𝔨-Ⅎⅽꞁꞁꞇⅽꞁꞇ

"IF I POINT TO Jane Austen, Dickens, Balzac, George Eliot, Tolstoy, Dostoevsky, the Melville of *Moby Dick*, Proust, the Joyce of *Ulysses*, Dreiser, Faulkner," writes Mary McCarthy, "it will be admitted that they are all novelists and that, different as they are from a formal point of view, they have one thing in common: a deep love of fact, of the empiric element in experience."[1] Later she suggests how essential this empiric element is to readers of novels. "If we read a novel, say, about conditions in postwar Germany, we expect it to be an accurate report of conditions in postwar Germany; if we find out that it is not, the novel is discredited. This is not the case with a play or a poem. Dante can be wrong in *The Divine Comedy*; it does not matter, with Shakespeare, that Bohemia has no seacoast, but if Tolstoy was all wrong about the Battle of Borodino or the character of Napoleon, *War and Peace* would suffer."[2] The conclusions that Mary McCarthy ultimately derives from these assumptions seem to me disputable. She suggests a sharp decline in the interest in fact among readers

[1]*On The Contrary* (New York: Farrar, Straus & Cudahy, 1961), p. 251.
[2]Ibid., p. 263.

of fiction. (Consider, for a single counterexample, the critical and popular success of E. L. Doctorow's *Ragtime*, which is "documentary" and evocative in some classic ways.) I cite the premises of her essay, however, because they are so firmly and gracefully stated; I take them to be indisputable. The main stream of the novel *is* fact-centered and we ordinarily expect a novelist to be totally and persuasively faithful to the verifiable world.

It is, of course, not simply fact qua fact that characterizes the novel but its remarkable fusion of fact with lie, its freedom of invention superimposed upon a base of authenticity. A whole history of the novel could be made of those two contrary but integrated impulses. Fielding, at all points, seeks to persuade us that *Tom Jones* is a work of the imagination, obedient to its own laws, "artificial," arranged, "made up." Yet Fielding composed his time scheme with almanac and calendar; he anchored the action historically to the invasion from Scotland in 1745; he copied Ralph Allen's house in describing Allworthy's; and he took obvious pains to get the feel of Somersetshire and London right. To leap centuries, Joyce's *Ulysses* is artifice and invention; it is evident that its first chapter issues not from some verifiable events in a Martello tower but from some plausible events within the imagination of Joyce. But there was—and still is—a Martello tower. And Joyce's famous letters to his Aunt Josephine requesting information about places in Dublin ("I want that information about the Star of the Sea Church, has it ivy on its seafront, are there trees in Leahy's terrace at the side or near, if so, what are these steps leading down to the beach?"[3]) testify to his passion for getting the facts right.

A different way of sensing the relation between these classic polarities and a different use of fact and the illusion

[3]*Letters of James Joyce*, ed. Stuart Gilbert (New York: Viking, 1957), p. 136.

of fact have subtly and unobtrusively appeared in recent years. I call it "mock-fact." Analogues exist in earlier literature. Swift's prediction of the death of Partridge the astrologer, his description of the event and its aftermath, Partridge himself remaining alive the whole time, is an analogue. But it is also an anomaly. Students of the eighteenth century read Swift's pamphlets now not as being characteristic of the eighteenth-century imagination but as being a special exercise in Swift's unusual wit. Virginia Woolf's *Orlando* is, in some respects, an exercise in mock-fact. And modernists in general, Woolfians in particular, hardly know what to do with it. Mock-fact, on the contrary, is not anomalous in the seventies but central to the purposes of postmodern fiction. And, although we may not know quite what to do with it, it is important that we make the effort.

Rather than defining, I begin by citing some very different but parallel examples. In Argentina in 1933, Borges wrote about Billy the Kid in a piece entitled "The Disinterested Killer Bill Harrigan." (It is significant of mock-fact that one doesn't know what besides *piece* to call the passages of prose in which it occurs: essays? articles? extended ironies? fictions? *ficciones*? parodies? spoofs? put-ons? stories?) The section called "The Larval Stage" goes like this:

> Along about 1859, the man who would become known to terror and glory as Billy the Kid was born in a cellar room of a New York City tenement. It is said that he was spawned by a tired-out Irish womb but was brought up among Negroes. In this tumult of lowly smells and wooly heads, he enjoyed a superiority that stemmed from having freckles and a mop of red hair. He took pride in being white; he was also scrawny, wild, and coarse. At the age of twelve, he fought in the gang of the Swamp Angels, that branch of divinities who operated among the neighborhood sewers. On nights redolent of burnt fog, they would clamber out of the foul-smelling labyrinth, trail some German sailor, do

him in with a knock on the head, strip him to his under-
wear, and afterward sneak back to the filth of their starting
place. Their leader was a gray-haired Negro, Gas House
Jonas, who was also celebrated as a poisoner of horses.[4]

Or, I quote from the beginning of "'Franz Kafka' by Jorge
Luis Borges" by Alvin Greenberg.

There is a story by Borges which neither you nor anyone
else has ever read, for it was written in the dialect of a remote Andean Indian Tribe among whom Borges lived
briefly while young, but whose language no one else knows.
Borges himself seems to have little memory of the language
at this late date; with his failing eyesight he can no longer
decipher the curious symbols which he has used to represent it on the printed page; and no one else either knows
what sounds the symbols were supposed to represent or
would be likely to pronounce them properly if he did.[5]

Or from the beginning of "The Geography of Ohio," by
Howard McCord:

Ohio lies fifteen thousand feet below sea level in a great rift
valley bisecting the western portion of the northeastern
corridor. The border with Indiana is considered by some
impassible, and by all as rivalled only by lunar structures of
yet undetermined origin. A stone dropped from Pennsyl-
vania does not land in Ohio, but in Indiana, the prevailing
upwardly westerlies prohibiting all but a few major airlines
from landing anything in Ohio.[6]

Or from a section of Jack Anderson's "Abandoned Cities"
called "Bismarck, North Dakota":

There are no suburbs. The streets stop at the wheatfields,
where the iron helmets are set on black sticks to frighten off
eagles. Beyond this point, the wind begins, as hard to ig-

[4]Jorge Luis Borges, *A Universal History of Infamy*, trans. Norman
Thomas di Giovanni (New York: Dutton, 1972), pp. 61–62.
[5]*New American Review* 8:155.
[6]*Fiction International* 23:121.

nore as stomach-ache. The townspeople fear two things always: drought and frost.[7]

Or from an annalistic account by Woody Allen of the trials of Lord Sandwich in attempting to invent the sandwich:

> 1745: After four years of frenzied labor, he is convinced he is on the threshold of success. He exhibits before his peers two slices of turkey with a slice of bread in the middle. His work is rejected by all but David Hume, who senses the imminence of something great and encourages him. Heartened by the philosopher's friendship, he returns to work with renewed vigor.[8]

Or from the beginning of Howard Moss's *Instant Lives*, a life of El Greco:

> "Why not make a virtue out of a defect, El?" the kindly eye doctor asked, bending over the artistic boy. Or should it be "autistic," the doctor thought to himself. The boy's eyes were not only hopelessly astigmatic, but a peculiarity, unique to the doctor's experience and probably genetic in origin, had elongated the lenses of the irises so that El Greco saw every object in the world attentuated to the point of emaciation. It was as if some abstract giant had pulled the taffy of reality out as far as it would stretch from both ends simultaneously, and then let it snap.[9]

Finally, I quote from the single piece of mock-fact that seems to me to put us more in touch with our own raw nerves than anything in the mode that I know, Donald Barthelme's "Robert Kennedy Saved From Drowning," this, a section entitled "Dress":

> He is neatly dressed in a manner that does not call attention to itself. The suits are soberly cut and in dark colors. He must be at all times present an aspect of freshness difficult to sustain because of frequent movements from place to

[7]*TriQuarterly* 18 (1970):20.
[8]*Getting Even* (New York: Warner Paperback Library, 1972), p. 34.
[9]Saturday Review Press (New York: Dutton, 1974), p. 33.

place under conditions which are not always the most favorable. Thus he changes clothes frequently, especially shirts. In the course of a day he changes his shirt many times. There are always extra shirts about, in boxes.

"Which of you has the shirts?"[10]

I have taken the risk of making what seems a small anthology, because something of the cumulative force, the ingenuity, and the energy of the mode need to be seen if my discussion is to rest on a substantial experience of its possibilities. Examples, as I have tried to suggest by my selection, can be found in the work of writers of world eminence and writers of no fame at all, writers at the ends of their careers and writers at the beginning, work in the major creative outlets of our time and work in obscure journals. What the examples have in common is a sense of gaiety and joy and a conflation of the factual and the fictive in a rather special way, so as to adopt the tones, the syntax, and the rhetorical orientations of factual prose while converting those rhetorical possibilities to a kind of mad invention.

The first thing to determine is what the new literature of mock-fact is not, since it is not, I think, really like anything we know. It is not parody, even though, as I suggest, the word comes to mind and relations to the parodic tradition are obvious. Whatever else parody may do, it imitates, with stylized exaggerations, a work or an author, allowing the force of its ingenuity to illuminate and undercut the style and manner of the original. None of my citations do exactly that, being diffuse and elusive in the objects of their imitation, if it is, in fact, satiric imitation which they pursue at all. Parody, moreover, implies a mixed tone: admiration of the author parodied and amusement at his expense. Beerbohm, for example, would be inconsiderable if he did

[10]*Unspeakable Practices, Unnatural Acts* (New York: Bantam, 1969), p. 33.

not genuinely admire the authors he mocks. But in my examples there is very little of that classic bipolar ambivalence. Burlesque is an even less applicable category, since there are no directly rendered social action, no farcical characters, no ridicule of social pieties; if Gilbert and Sullivan operettas are acceptable models of burlesque, it is hard to see that they have anything in common with the examples I cite. Irony may, in the long run, be an illuminating category. The examples are all, in some broad and devious way, ironic. But in the plain sense in which one might speak of my examples as being "ironies," exercises in saying roughly the opposite of what is meant while cuing the reader so as to induce him to understand what *is* meant, in that sense the examples do nothing of the kind. What the opposite of Borges's assertions about Billy the Kid would be is impossible to say. And nobody, I assume, rushes to a gazetteer, after reading Jack Anderson's piece, to determine the verifiable facts about Bismarck by way of appreciating the contrary inventions of Anderson.

The whole range of possibilities for which the phrase *put-on* is a convenient designation are treated in the *locus classicus* for discussion of the phenomenon, Jacob Brackman's brilliant essay, first published in the *New Yorker*, later published separately, entitled *The Put-on: Modern Fooling and Modern Mistrust*. Early in the essay, Brackman establishes the kinship between the modern put-on and older forms of kidding or hoaxing, along with the differences between them. "The object of kidding, as of hoaxing," he writes, "is always manifest: to *pass off* untruth as truth just for the fun of it."[11] Kidding and hoaxing depend upon a stable truth which is known to the perpetrator, concealed from the victim, and finally revealed. In the case of the put-on, however, the intent is ambiguous, the motive

[11](New York: Bantam, 1972), p. 18.

unclear, and the "truth" that would presumably correct the apparent exaggerations is not revealed—if, in fact, it exists—leaving us with the suspicion that we have been tricked but with no way of confirming it. Examples come most easily to Brackman from either social conversation or the art world. "A famous artist is comissioned to paint the portrait of, say, Mrs. Felice Worthingham. 'I'm very busy,' he mutters. 'Let's see. . . .' He writes the words 'Portrait of Mrs. Felice Worthingham' on a grubby torn-off piece of paper. Then he signs the jotting and hands it over to Mrs. Worthingham, who has the 'portrait' framed and pays the artist's usual fee—five thousand dollars."[12]

Brackman finds more reasons to deplore the put-on, both in its social and its aesthetic manifestations, than he finds reasons to applaud it. It is a strategy that provides a refuge for the untalented, a facile substitute for the craft and the demands of art, a dodge by means of which a voguish cleverness can be substituted for thought. The literature of mock-fact thrives, obviously, in a culture in which the sensibility of the put-on prevails as it does in ours. But again, it seems to me that the category of the put-on confuses more than it illuminates, if we extend it to include the literature of mock-fact. Brackman's comments on the absence of craft apply easily enough to an Andy Warhol film of a man sleeping for eight hours. They do not apply to a prose piece by Borges, as tight, artful, controlled, and precise in its language as any prose now written. Neither do Brackman's remarks on the elusiveness of intention and the confusion of response that occur in the put-on apply to the literature of mock-fact.

Whatever "The Geography of Ohio" may be intended to do, it is not intended to fool anyone. The reader who knows nothing about the geography of Ohio knows, from the first

[12] Ibid., p. 17.

sentence, that he is in the country of the mind. And if he reads on, it is not as uneasy victim but as a willing participant in an act of the imagination. It is possible, perhaps, to imagine a reader of Alvin Greenberg's piece who knows nothing of Borges, who misses the connection between Borges's own work and Greenberg's, and who is taken in by the apparent earnestness of Greenberg's prose. But there are variations in the responsiveness of readers to anything. And there is no reason to believe that Greenberg is writing to *that* reader, hoping to put him on, but rather he is writing to the reader who knows enough to assume, immediately, that the material is fiction, without attempt to deceive.

Not really like anything we know, mock-fact is close enough to all of those familiar modes, such as parody and put-on, that it seems not particularly audacious or experimental. Yet it alters the traditional equipoise between the empirical world and the novelist's invention in a new way. And, in fact, it even uses language in a way different from other fiction.

The novel always seeks to find and present a relationship between the prior world, in the Mary McCarthy sense of history and fact, and the invented world of the characters, who may be, variously, typical, or loosely suggestive of some principle or trait larger than themselves, or plainly illustrative, or exemplary, or allegorical, characters who bear some kind of blend of the individual and the schematic, who both *are* and *mean*. It is this blend that we speak of when we refer to the novelist's having made a world, a fusion of the historical and the imagined, the public world and the private, the quotidian and the schematized, the conditions of life as they are available to any observing mind and the conditions of life transformed by the intellectual and moral vision of the novelist. Nearly every experiment with fiction leaves that base intact. The experimenter may alter syntax and linguistic order; he may transform time, space, and causality; he may transmute perceptual modes and virtually reinvent the human image. But for all this, he still invents a world. Hawkes, Kosinski, Coover, and Pynchon make worlds just as surely as Richardson, Dickens, Balzac, and Stendhal did.

What is so radically innovative about mock-fact, then, is that it does not make a world. It neither makes statements about the historical world, in the manner of certain passages of Tolstoy, nor does it make statements about the imagined world of a group of characters, in the manner of most of Jane Austen. It pretends to make statements of fact, about the historical and verifiable world, yet contrives to make them in such a way as to make clear to the reader that the statements in no way assert anything about the world at all. From the reader's point of view, mock-fact neither invites us to believe in the historicity of its assertions, as we believe Tolstoy, nor to assent to the interior logical and imaginative coherence of the projected world, as we do with Jane Austen. What mock-fact does, in short, is to make fiction that denies the very fictive impulse. "Emma was not required, by any subsequent discovery, to retract her ill opinion of Mrs. Elton," writes Jane Austen. "Her observation had been pretty correct. Such as Mrs. Elton appeared to her on this second interview, such she appeared whenever they met again,—self-important, presuming, familiar, ignorant, and ill-bred." What we are required to do as we read those lines is to assent to the credibility of Emma, to believe in the general accuracy with which the rhythms of leisured life in 1800 are represented, to will ourselves into a world in which the moral and social imperatives used of Mrs. Elton have all of the point and force Emma means them to have, and to believe in the stylistic and imaginative intelligence with which that passage stands in relation to the whole vision of the novel.

"There are no suburbs," writes Jack Anderson. "The streets stop at the wheatfields, where the iron helmets are set on black sticks to frighten off eagles." What we are required to do as we read those lines is *not* assent to the credibility of the speaker, *not* believe in the layout of the streets, the iron helmets, the eagles, *not* believe that essential representations are being made of life in the American great plains, *not* believe in the validity of the imaginative vision of which those lines form a part, at least not in any sense that we have already learned.

What mock-fact does ask us to do is to join a conspiracy to transcend banality. The one common element of all of my selections is that they address themselves to banal subjects: the childhood of Billy the Kid; the possibility of a lost, early, ignorable story by Borges in an unreadable language; the geography of Ohio; the geography of Bismarck, North Dakota; the invention of the sandwich; El Greco's first trip to the ophthalmologist; and Robert Kennedy's wardrobe. Having addressed the banal, they then present us with models of the imaginative life, meeting and overcoming the world of sheer, dumb information. Each example uses devices, either of ordering the material or of diction and syntax, derived from the expository disciplines. But the point, I think, is not exactly to mock the disciplines themselves. Geography qua geography is not mocked by the two geographical passages. The point is rather to overcome the dull irrelevance of fact by the triumph of wit.

Two small examples from elsewhere can suggest what I mean. Readers of Pynchon's *V.* will recall the image of the alligators in the sewers of New York. One of the New York department stores once had a sale of baby alligators; New York children bought them, tired of them, and flushed them down their toilets, where they entered the sewer system, growing to maturity underground, blind and white. I have had the experience, several times, of alluding to that image and finding that people know the story, people who have never read *V.* or have heard the story before *V.* ever appeared. Evidently the idea was not an original one with Pynchon but was rather a piece of available folklore that he turned to his own novelistic purposes. I take it as axiomatic that the existence and durability of the story of the alligators in the sewers proves something of the power and pertinence of the story. There are, of course, no alligators in the sewers of New York. Most of those who have heard the story or told it themselves know it is not true. But it is told as if true, not with an intent to deceive but because it is better than the truth. It is a myth, which figures forth the mass response to mass commercial appeals in mass society, the almost automatic and predictable occurrence of boredom toward commercial novelties, the existence of a savage and unknown life underground. The story of the alligators could not be told effectively unless it were told with the illusion of fact. Having been told, it has the status of myth, truer than fact because it energizes a whole range of feelings about the most basic nature of our life in the world.

For another example, some years ago political satirist Art Buchwald wrote a column in which he maintained that J. Edgar Hoover did not exist, that purported photographs of him were clever composites, that the name was an invention of some idle wags in the F.B.I. office, and that the work he was alleged to have done was, when done at all, done by a committee. It was surely one of the most durable columns Buchwald ever wrote. One still finds allusions to it years after the death of Hoover and the writing of the column. One of the reasons for its success was the intricate consistency with which Buchwald worked out the plausible conditions under which a public, but very private, man could be imagined not to exist. But the more potent reason for its success was that it became an instant myth. The story, not true but told as if true, evoked a real feeling, universally shared, that well-known figures are media shadows, public relations figments, inventions of the culture, never seen in the flesh, without a life of their own, virtually without a verifiable existence.

The phenomenon of mock-fact has its outer limits, fiction of a kind that mimes not exactly the assertion of fact, as do the examples I have cited, but specialized discourse within the world of fact. Here, for example, is the beginning of a fiction that mimes the discourse that brings analytic methods, especially psychological and cultural methods, to bear upon pop artifacts, in this case films. "It is logical that having written at some length on King Kong I should turn to Tarzan of the Apes. There are many striking parallels. For example, their native habitat is jungle. Further, Tarzan, like Kong, seems unable to find his generative organ, or, if he has found it, seems equally unable to divine its function. Hence in both cases a good deal of sublimated sexuality in the form of encounters with wild beasts."[13] Quoting the beginning cannot suggest how ingeniously the piece is sustained and how it grows to become a very funny but also quite rich and resonant meditation, strange and haunting, independent of any parodic impulse merely to mock pretentious film criticism.

In another direction A. B. Paulson's "The Minnesota Multiphasic Personality: a diagnostic test in two parts" mimes the form of the standard personality test, with narrative sections, followed by interpretive multiple choice statements, all slightly preposterous, among which the reader is invited to choose, and confessional statements ("I want to throw my popcorn box at the screen"; "Never discuss your personal life with prospective employees") requiring a T or F response.[14] The form of Paulson's fiction

[13] Kenneth Bernard, "King Kong: A Meditation," *New American Review* 14:182.
[14] *TriQuarterly* 29 (1974):204–12.

duplicates the rigid rationality of the personality test, while its questions and choices reach down into the driven, paranoid, obsessional, hallucinatory, Angst-ridden world of the reader as test-taker. And so a fiction that seems to deny its fictionality accomplishes, in fact, a remarkable evocation of an area of experience which no conventional narrative could touch.

So it is that a kind of fiction, largely new, appears to deny all that is essential to the fictive act. It tells stories in an odd and sketchy way at best, often does not make stories at all. Often it masquerades as essay, or encyclopedia article, or biographical summary, or news-magazine report. As such, it invites us to mock the forms of factual assertion. Yet it does not exist for the purpose of formal mockery. It signals us at once that it carries no intention of asserting facts. Nor does it assert pseudofacts about an imagined world. What it does is to convert the forms by means of which facts are asserted to an altogether different kind of fictive act, which is at once playful and more than a little astonishing. There is, I think, no epistemological revolution involved. It is not that such fictions wish us to disbelieve in the possibility of fact—Bishop Berkeley *redivivus*. The mean elevation of the state of Ohio is what it is, and Howard McCord has no wish to challenge the legitimacy of the U.S. Coast and Geodetic Survey. Mock-fact, rather than an epistemological challenge, is an imaginative gesture. Hawthorne learned to tell stories about Puritan ministers, about whom nobody cares, so as to invest them with a significance that makes readers care. Dreiser learned to tell stories about working girls, about whom nobody cares, so as invest them with a significance that makes readers care. James learned to tell stories about homely heiresses, about whom nobody cares, so as to invest them with a significance that makes readers care. The history of fiction is the history of the transcendence of the banal. And mock-fact accomplishes the most stunning transcendence of them all, superimposing the myth-making imagination upon the plain, flat data of the world.

For a sense of the limitless possibilities of the form, one need only reflect on the extraordinary power of Barthelme's Robert Kennedy story: intricate and inventive, playful and self-aware, also in touch with our consciousness of the man, our inescapable tendency to see him through clouds of journalistic prose, the elaborate contrivance necessary to maintain his image, his terrible fragility. There will always be those who will find that the definitive biography, with a spine two inches thick, puts them most firmly in touch with their sense of the man himself. Barthelme, I think, has no quarrel with writers and readers of thick biographies, and for all I know reads them himself. But there is a way of imagining the man by the use of lies in the dress of dry fact that carries its own eccentric power to mean and extends the possibilities of fiction in our own fact-glutted age.

CHAPTER EIGHT

Satire without an Object

One of the functions of a publisher is, of course, to introduce books to the world, a function that is at once commercial and institutional. One means of doing this is by flap copy on a book's dust jacket, which undertakes to describe in a few sentences, with ingratiating warmth, the book's contents and to praise it in the words of the copy-writer or of somebody else. Also implicit in this task is the obligation to place the work in a class or tradition, to name the kind of thing it is. This falls back on the use of generic terminology, language that sooner or later makes everyone who uses it feel uncomfortable, be they critics or copywriters. But the language of classification is, after all, an irreducible necessity for the analytic intelligence, so we go on using it because we must. Here let us imagine that enterprise as it applies to new fiction, that institutional obligation to say the first words ever said about new novels, not only to praise, but also to place in context.

I suggest a series of fictions, extending over twenty years or so, for which one might imagine such a challenge to classify, briefly and glibly perhaps, but usefully, as a signal to the potential reader that the book he is holding in his

hand is, although unique, like certain other works that he
has read. *Catch-22*, for a first example, is stylized and ex-
travagant, mixed and various in its progress, quite obviously scornful of many of the aspects of the world it ren-
ders: consequently one might well decide that, whatever
else might be said of it, it could, with some legitimacy, for
purposes of a dust jacket blurb, be called a satire. *The Sot-
Weed Factor* conceivably generates the same response. So
does *Lolita*. So does *V*. So does Stanley Elkin's *Boswell*,
Jerome Charyn's *The Tar Baby*, Alan Friedman's *Herma-
phrodeity*, Barthelme's *Snow White*, and Alvin Greenberg's *The Invention of the West*.

Such a list might be extended many times. All of these
works, and many more, *look* like satires. Yet assume that
one, in the imaginary role as writer of flap copy, has called
them, publicly, in print, satires. To the audience for these
works, I suggest that the term is likely to seem unsatisfactory and inappropriate. It is too limiting, perhaps, or too
specific, suggesting that the works in question perpetuate
a tradition we associate with Lucian and Juvenal, Swift and
Pope, or suggesting a kind of pragmatic, directed emotional force in the works, as if the writers were instructing
us in the proper objects of our contempt, and nothing so
pragmatic seems to be happening in the contemporary
works we are reading.

The question implicit in the imperfect applicability of
the term *satire* to contemporary fiction concerns the relation between the implicit reference to a wider world within
the work, which is to say the *objects* of the satire, and the
responses of an attentive reader. This relation tends to be
examined, in the classic criticism on the subject, in an ideal
and mechanical way. However vexed the meaning of *Gul-
liver's Travels* may be, for example, it is clear how the work
functions when examined in this ideal way. Neither Gul-
liver nor the King of Brobdignag is a character. Both are

vehicles for the presentation of a more-or-less free play of events and judgments expressive of the amusement, scorn, and indignation of Swift toward English and European institutions, ultimately the very nature of man; and it is the responsibility of the reader to know enough of those institutions to be able to see through the narration to the objects of Swift's scorn. By calling such a description ideal or mechanical, I do not mean to imply that something like this does not happen. It is, in fact, an apt description of what often does happen. Nevertheless the rather complex and devious nature of satire and the imperatives of contemporary fiction, of the kind that I have named as having a curious resemblance to classic satire, both suggest the usefulness of adding to that classic description another approach that is perverse and eccentric.

A child of mine is reading a parody in *Mad* magazine on, let us say, *Clockwork Orange*. The movie is rated X, and he could not see it even if I wish to take him. He is a bright child but hardly spends his time reading reviews of movies he will never see. He laughs at the parody—of a movie he has not seen, knows little about, and never hopes to see. "What are you laughing at," asks his rationalistic father, "since you haven't seen the movie?" The question reduces the child to semiarticulate revolt, and it is right that it should. What answer could satisfy the question? Did I want him to cite Hobbes? Freud? Bergson? The question is obviously beyond analysis for the child and, to some extent, for myself. I would suggest, incidentally, that the relationship between the satiric intention and response of the audience represented by my child's reading of *Mad* is emblematic of vast areas of popular culture: the wish to express a diffuse mockery that registers on audiences as a generalized and indeterminate disdain. Consider the fact that night club and television mimics continue to do imitations of James Cagney and Edward G. Robinson, parodying roles they played in films of forty years ago, for the appreciative amusement of audiences often in their teens and twenties, almost none of whom have seen the movies and many of whom could not even name the actor being mocked.

Hardly confined to the bright and responsive but uninformed imagination of a child, such readings of satire are commonplace among readers of any age or education. Among classic satiric works, Pope's *Dunciad* provides the clearest example of a split between informed and uninformed readings. To a scholar, everything is necessary for a proper reading of Pope's poem: Pope's notes, Warburton's notes, the Twickenham edition's notes, as well as a compendious knowledge of the eighteenth century in general and its literary quarrels in particular. But to W. H. Auden and Norman Holmes Pearson, in their introduction to *Restoration and Augustan Poets*, "*The Dunciad* is not only a great poem but also the only poem in English which is at once comic and sublime. It should never be read with notes, for to think that it matters who the characters were or why Pope was angry with them is to miss the whole point of the poem, which is best appreciated by supplying one's own contemporary list of the servants of the Goddess of Dullness." While it is easy to dismiss the Auden-Pearson opinion as being dilettantish, it is wrong to do so. The reading they propose has been given to the poem by a large proportion of readers over the years, many of whom are possessed of taste and education. And while that reading is, in some respects, less rich and dense than the scholar's, it may, on the other hand, permit an imaginative participation in the spirit of the satire that the fully informed reader can never again find.

Satire that strikes the mind of an audience which *knows* the object of that satire creates a set of responses which begin with the social and extend to the intellectual. It is a

process of learning to like, or learning to dislike, certain
people, and, as a consequence, to like, or dislike, certain
ideas and intellectual postures. The ideal reader, or spec-
tator, of *Tartuffe* comes away with a reinvigorated distaste
for religious hypocrites, a literary response analogous to
the social process of making friends and enemies. That
quasi-social response results, of course, from seeing, or
reading, the speeches of one highly particularized example, in a concretely rendered social setting. Along the
way, the reader extends the response to a dislike for religious hypocrisy, perhaps even for the hypocritical possibilities latent in all religion, an intellectual generalizing inevitable when one knows what the satire is about. For the
reader who knows the object of the satire, it is never possible to reconstitute the apparent emotional intent of the
author. If the author was indignant when he wrote, no
reader will be indignant. If the author was withdrawn and
condescending, mocking dryly from his Horatian retreat,
no reader will do just that as he reads. Instead, the reader
who knows the object of the satire will detach himself one
degree above both victim and satirist, being amused at the
object in its foolishness and involved in an uneasy relationship with the satirist, never as angry as the satirist, occasionally, in fact, amused at the satirist in his rage, yet feeling a kinship with him, against fools and knaves. And it is
this complicated relationship with the satirist that prompts
the learned reader, who wishes to know all he can about
Pope's dunces, to know also all he can about Pope. Such, I
suggest, is the quintessential experience of the reader who
understands the butt: his primary response is quasi-social,
his secondary response is intellectual, and his emotional
stance is low-keyed amusement.

On the other hand, satire that strikes the mind of an audience which *does not know* the object of the satire creates
a set of responses that begin with the formal and extend to

the cultural. At the formal level, matters of timing and fluidity, distortion, misproportion, and misapplication are salient. To a person who does not recognize the figures referred to, any editorial cartoon is still potent art, with its swelled heads, its bulbous noses, the pompous ineffectuality, the smug complacency, the dumb frustration written on every face. Even if one could imagine a person who did not know that Herblock's Nixon represented Nixon, that drawing would still be amusing, the hunched shoulders, the scowl, the swooping nose, the five o-clock shadow, the jowls. So it is with literary satire. If one could somehow imagine reading it as pure fable, without reference to Leibniz and eighteenth-century optimism, without reference to prevailing philosophy at all, without reference to the historical world of the eighteenth century, *Candide* would be a potent book, its energy and inventiveness evident in every line. It may well be, in fact, that a reader of a satire who has no sense of its reference may have a richer sense of its formal ingenuity, the movement of its rhythms, the distortion of its forms, since the diverse parade of its human images is then the sole concern, unencumbered by any interest in what it is all ultimately *about*.

Now let me take the argument a step further. It is possible, I suggest, for a writer to write what looks like satire, what feels to the reader like satire, what repeats all of the formal strategies of satire, and yet not mean it to be about the specific folly of the world, in a sense not to be about anything but itself. It is as if the writer, acknowledging the legitimacy of the naïve reading of satire that I describe, set out to make such a reading the only one possible. Or, to put it another way, it is as if a staff cartoonist for *Mad* composed a parody, following all the conventions for parody, the stylized postures, the clichés, yet composed the parody about no movie that ever existed.

Max Apple's story "The Oranging of America" begins in this way:

> From the outside it looked like any ordinary 1964 Cadillac limousine. In the expensive space between the driver and passengers, where some installed bars or even bathrooms, Mr. Howard Johnson kept a tidy ice-cream freezer in which there were always at least eighteen flavors on hand, though Mr. Johnson ate only vanilla. The freezer's power came from the battery with an independent auxiliary generator as a back-up system. Although now Howard Johnson means primarily motels, Millie, Mr. HJ, and Otis Brighton, the chauffeur, had not forgotten that ice cream was the cornerstone of their empire. Some of the important tasting was still done in the car.[1]

It suddenly seems quite legitimate, once Apple has done it, to take a corporation, such as Howard Johnson's, which happens to retain a personal name, and to imagine its founder functioning, tasting ice cream, riding in his limousine, soliciting the judgment of his chauffeur. The narration is deadpan and flat, the situation is stylized and grotesque. And consequently the passage looks like satire. Yet one looks in vain for a level of reference implicit in the narration, that area of the experiential world toward which the narration could conceivably point with amusement and scorn. A reader who expected the narration to be directed toward American mass culture in general and the uniform food of restaurant chains in particular would be making a reasonable guess. Or the reader who expected the narration to be directed toward the curious disjunction between the old-style American entrepreneur, a living, breathing human being with passions and eccentricities, and the corporate machine that his passion engenders would also be making a legitimate guess. But Apple's story, as it pro-

[1] *The Oranging of America and Other Stories* (New York: Grossman, 1976), p. 3.

ceeds, never implicitly points us toward either level of reference. The story is a free invention growing out of certain observations on American life. But its *about*ness is self-contained. It is satire without an object.

Almost any passage from Pynchon will yield the same results. Consider these lines from *V.*

> Next evening, prime and nervous-thighed in a rear seat of the crosstown bus, Esther divided her attention between the delinquent wilderness outside and a paperback copy of *The Search for Bridey Murphy.* This book had been written by a Colorado businessman to tell people there was life after death. In its course he touched upon metempsychosis, faith healing, extrasensory perception and the rest of a weird canon of twentieth-century metaphysics we've come now to associate with the city of Los Angeles and similar regions.
>
> The bus driver was of the normal or placid crosstown type; having fewer traffic lights and stops to cope with than the up-and-downtown drivers, he could afford to be genial. A portable radio hung by his steering wheel, turned to WQXR. Tchaikovsky's Romeo and Juliet Overture flowed syrupy around him and his passengers.[2]

A stylized treatment of American cults and the beginnings of a stylized treatment of Manhattan life, the passage looks satiric. Yet the treatment of American interest in the occult does not exist to figure forth an implicit level of reference to which the reader is expected to respond so as to join the author in amusement and scorn. The cultishness is simply there, a part of the primary data of the fiction. And there is no "object" beyond the lines on the page.

As with so much of what I have tried to isolate and find ways of reading in contemporary fiction, satire without an object is prominent now in a way in which it never was before, but it is less new than it seems. Reading back from

[2](New York: Bantam, 1964), p. 83.

Faulkner's Nobel Prize acceptance speech, for example, or from his numerous interviews and the transcripts of his classes at the University of Virginia, one would look in vain for an intentional gloss that would account for the stroke of genius by means of which he came to name one of his characters Montgomery Ward Snopes. It is a fictional choice, the discovery of that wonderful name, that has nothing to do with those classic ways in which Faulkner and other novelists, and critics in their wake, have explained their motives and justified their works, nothing to do, that is, with the tradition of the novel, nothing to do with the imitation of life, and nothing to do with morality, although once Montgomery Ward Snopes is fleshed out and put in motion, of course, he has something to do with all three of these. But *that choice*, the decision to endow him with that memorable name, results in a moment in which observed "reality" is pulled and stretched, stylized and energized, a moment that is of the nature of satire perhaps, like giving a doctor in a farce a name suggestive of pain and neglect, but is finally without an object, a stylized moment consistent with the vulgarity of the Snopses but lacking that directed pragmatic intention which we rightly associate with satire. So it is throughout the tradition of prose fiction, a tradition filled with characters, styles, and events that have about them the bizarre extravagance which signals the apparent intention to mock but do so, if at all, with the weakest of will, allowing their mad inventiveness to be its own justification.

Quevedo at one end of the history of fiction, Günter Grass at the other exemplify the tendency I describe. Between them, among our classics, are Smollett and Dickens, both of whom will congratulate themselves for their moral seriousness and their truth to experience, neither of whom will congratulate himself for that amazing extravagance which exists everywhere in his work not in pursuit of a

satiric point but for itself. A cluster of pivotal books have
marked the transition to a mode of fiction in which that
free, stylized invention now is as central as it is. The best
example of these works is *Lolita.*

Nabokov begins with a mock preface by John Ray, Jr.,
claiming mimetic fidelity and moral purpose in the novel
to follow; Nabokov ends the work with his own afterword,
"On a Book Entitled *Lolita,*" disavowing any such purposes. Between preface and afterword exist all of those
American mothers and American daughters, American mo-
tels and American restaurants, American summer camps
and American suburbs for which the book is justly famous,
all of them demonstrating considerable vulgarity yet none
of them existing for the purpose of mocking that vulgarity
so as to implicitly assert certain standards of decency and
taste.

That fiction has come to elevate the possibilities of what
I have called *satire without an object* seems both inevitable
and overdue. Why it has happened at this particular point
has something to do with the relations between author and
reader. Rhetorically, satire always assumes a willingness by
the audience to conspire in the game, to perform that necessary act of generalizing and reading-through that I have
argued is difficult or impossible in contemporary fiction. It
is not only avowedly satiric writers who construct an implicit pact with their readers. Novelists from Fielding to
Thackeray play directly to the best and worst of an audience they know intimately. And modernist writers, no matter how dense and devious, always assume an audience,
however small, that will meet the demands of their art
with, if necessary, a lifetime of study. Commentary by nontraditional contemporary writers on the nature and prob-
able response of their audience is, on the other hand, extremely rare. One can read through volume after volume
of such fiction without any sense of whom these writers

think they are writing *for*. And the absence of such a preexistent sense of audience seems to me to have something to do with the unlikelihood that serious, sustained prose fiction can exist based upon the assumption that an audience will receive the literature, making all of the necessary exegetical moves, so as to arrive at the shared indignation that gives satire its reason for being. It is a rhetorical impasse that Vonnegut expresses nicely at the end of an interview.

> There's my state representative. I campaigned for him, and he got drunk one night and came over and said, "You know, I can't understand a word you write and neither can any of your neighbors . . . so why don't you change your style, so why not write something people will like?" He was just telling me for my own good. He was a former English major at Brown.

"Did he win?" asks the interviewer. And Vonnegut replies: "He went crazy. He really went bughouse, finally."[3]

It is not only the loss of a community of readers that accounts for the mode I describe but also the loss of a shared iconography. Satire has most often been an urban art, using the vulgar, faceless crowd as the setting for its most potent effects. Satire has most often been antifeminist, finding women intrinsically ridiculous. And it has most often been sexually conservative, finding images of deviation from monogamous heterosexuality easy objects of scorn. After centuries of usefulness, these three areas of imagery are at last played out, and a writer in quest of conventional images to signal his readers that it is time to focus their scorn will find that our own areas of discontent are deeper and more diffuse than those traditional images will permit. Petronius found that the ostentatious display

[3]Joe David Bellamy, *The New Fiction: Interviews with Innovative American Writers* (Urbana: University of Illinois Press, 1974), pp. 206–7.

of food by the vulgar rich was so useful an image for demonstrating their lack of taste that he used Trimalchio's banquet as the central event of *The Satyricon*; centuries later, Flaubert, wishing to satirize the vulgarity of the rural gentry, used an ostentatious wedding feast. However much remains of class antagonisms and the wish to mock the nouveau riche, the ostentatious meal no longer serves as a shared focal point for such feelings. It too is played out. Our discontents are more general. And thus a range of invention that is nontraditional and nonconventional is more likely to express our sense of experience than that mode which sought for centuries to focus negative judgments by means of a largely inherited and continuous body of images.

It is finally in the sense of the world implicit in the vision of contemporary fiction, however, that satire without an object most firmly justifies itself. In conventional satire, the world is dualistic. There are those who are knaves and fools, and there are those who are neither. There is bad taste and good taste. There is madness, irrationality, and destructive passion; and there is sanity, sweet reason, and benevolence. In contemporary fiction that dualism largely disappears. There is the grotesque without the vision of a perfection of form, irrationality without the possibility of reason, bad taste without the possibility of good taste.

Perhaps this position is best expressed by that splendid precursor of the fiction I have been attempting to describe, Nathanael West. The images of West's fiction are grotesque in the manner of satire, and among them is no relief, no norm, no intermittent figure who can be taken to stand for sanity and good taste. Writing to a friend, West describes the way in which his fiction seems to alienate "the radical press," "the literature boys," "the highbrow press," even his successive publishers. "There is nothing to root for in my

work," he ends, "and what is even worse, no rooters."[4] It is
a description of the fiction of the seventies, a fiction informed by the satirist's eye and the satirist's narrative techniques, fond of the narrative energy that turns itself to a
satirist's excess, yet uninformed by the normative judgments that give us clear objects, discriminations, dualities,
something "to root for."

If I have described satire without an object by a series of
negatives, by what it is not, implying that fiction now represents a sense of loss, that is not the impression I wish
finally to leave. The absence of a pragmatic, traditional focus is at once a loss and a liberation. Joseph Heller's prose
can stand as a last exhibit, demonstrating, to my taste at
least, the pleasures and the power of a free invention that
looks like satire but elevates its own stylized vision above
its author's wish to direct our judgments.

> Yossarian shook his head. He sat nude on the lowest limb
> of the tree and balanced himself with both hands grasping
> the bough directly above. He refused to budge, and Milo
> had no choice but to stretch both arms about the trunk in a
> distasteful hug and start climbing. He struggled upward
> clumsily with loud grunts and wheezes, and his clothes
> were squashed and crooked by the time he pulled himself
> up high enough to hook a leg over the limb and pause for
> breath. . . . Yossarian watched him impassively. Cautiously
> Milo worked himself around in a half circle so that he could
> face Yossarian. He unwrapped tissue paper from something
> soft, round and brown and handed it out to Yossarian.
> "Please taste this and let me know what you think. I'd
> like to serve it to the men."
> "What is it?" asked Yossarian, and took a big bite.
> "Chocolate-covered cotton."[5]

[4]Quoted in Richard B. Gehman, "Nathanael West: A Novelist Apart,"
Atlantic 186 (Sept. 1950):72.
[5]*Catch-22* (New York: Dell, 1962), p. 268.

CHAPTER NINE

Prolegomena to
the Study of Fictional Dreck

ᗷ⅄ᗷⱯ *(mirrored duplicate of title)*

MOST NEW FICTION IN THE UNITED STATES that is innovative in form and sensibility is also comic. Readers of American fiction, in fact, may well be so accustomed to thinking of experimental motives and forms as being consistent with comic appeals that it may seem to us inevitable that the two should coexist. It is not, of course, inevitable at all. Most of the great works of Modernism are comic, if at all, only incidentally. Nobody laughs at *To the Lighthouse* or *Swann's Way* or *Nausea* or *The Sound and the Fury*. Nor is it even true that most postmodernist experimental fiction is comic. The French have given a whole generation in mid-twentieth century to certain kinds of fictional experimentation, most of it relentlessly serious. Much of Robbe-Grillet is played out against the very edge of lunacy; yet for the most part the only reader who laughs at the reading of a Robbe-Grillet novel is the reader who laughs at Robbe-Grillet. So it is that, although the American narrative literature that is nontraditional and antirealistic in the last twenty years is also most often comic, the one aspect is not a necessary condition of the other, and the nature of the comic appeal is not self-evident but problematic.

Experimental fiction is, by its very nature, uncircumscribed and anticonventional. So there must always be a range of effects at work in such fiction that defies orderly explanation. Yet there is a center to the comedy of experimental fiction, a common concern, a common set of images, or a common metaphor for the experience of the seventies as that experience is rendered in new fiction. This shared characteristic derives from certain attitudes toward, and treatments of, the shared mass-cultural objects of our world, especially the ephemeral objects, the floating junk, the jingles and slogans of advertising, the clichés of our common cant, the songs of forgotten hit parades, the faded movies, the throw-away plastic things, the receding but still talking faces of the TV screen, the disconnected items of schlock merchandise bought and unused, the mounting trash—in a word, the *dreck*[1] of our lives.

It is not self-evident how the use of dreck should be comic. A beer can by the highway is not funny; neither is an old shoe on a trash heap, nor coffee grounds in the garbage. Neither is it self-evident what any of this has to do with the innovative, antirealist, experimental motives of the writers I have cited. Nor is it self-evident that such material is new to fiction, since we tend to think of realist fiction from Defoe as being defined by the prominence it gives to sharply realized, comparatively nonsignificant de-

[1] It is Barthelme who has given the word *dreck* the currency it now has. But the word also survives because of its special resonance. The tone of the Yiddish word seems just right for its use in the senses I develop in this chapter, a back-of-the-hand scorn coupled with a good-natured amusement. But best of all, it means more than any English word, with a range of connotations extending from the excremental (the English *crap*) through trash, junk, garbage, all the way to shoddy merchandise and tasteless objects.

tails. Yet the use of trash is, in a certain context, all of these—funny, experimental, and new—as I hope to illustrate in the short run and to demonstrate in the long run. To illustrate, in a fiction by Steve Katz called "Oedipus," which is a revision and a boisterous vulgarization of the Oedipus myth, the protagonist puts out his eyes with a Py-Co-Pay toothbrush. The brand name in that context is indisputably comic—if not experimental, at least nontraditional, and a use of detail inconceivable in an earlier writer.

I take *Madame Bovary* as being the quintessential nineteenth-century realistic novel, a legitimate base for considering how fiction has come to be the thing it is. Flaubert begins his second part with a chapter describing Yonville. It begins geographically, with town names, descriptions of roads, names of rivers. Much of the description is rather remarkably cinematic, with the eye moving from pastures to plains to hills to horizon. It is a world both picturesque and suggestive of its backward agricultural economy. Flaubert moves us closer to the center of town and begins to register the outbuildings, the houses, the architectural details, and ultimately a few decorative details. Inevitably, both for Flaubert and for Yonville, the church is described with particularity and scorn. There is the market. There is Homais's pharmacy. The description of the town is finished with a paragraph that describes the cemetery beyond its edge in which the sexton uses the spare ground to plant potatoes.

Imagine a writer now in search of the images that would body forth small-town vulgarity. I suggest a few. A Coca Cola sign. A Dr. Pepper sign. The name of the local newspaper. A McDonald's hamburger stand surrounded by time-killing teenagers. A movie theater, plaster-Moorish in style, now boarded up. A bus station. A tourist court with separate cabins. An automobile parts store that seems to

specialize in chrome-plated tail pipes. Obviously I am se-
lecting details from twentieth-century America, not nineteenth-century provincial France. But my point is that the
imagination now turns easily and naturally to the commercial images, the neon signs, and the cheap diners that per-
vade small towns, and that these are, for us, the iconography for the poverty of spirit which we find there. For
Flaubert, no such commercial imagery comes to mind. Except for some quaint patent medicines listed in script on
Homais's pharmacy, nothing in Yonville seems to be bought
or sold. Despite the rural character of the town, the in-
habitants' lives must have been filled with vulgar and
trashy merchandise, most of it tasteless and some of it
mass-produced. Yet Flaubert does not see that particular
kind of trash, useful though it might have been to his purpose, preferring instead to define the vulgarity of Yonville
by describing the potato patch in the cemetery.

    Consider a parallel situation in nineteenth-century
England. Of that brilliant galaxy of prophets—Ruskin,
Morris, Carlyle, Arnold, Pater (and in America Emerson
and Thoreau)—a painful awareness of the nature of mass-
produced objects is central to the analysis of all of them.
Yet one searches in vain in the fiction of the period for that
pervasive consciousness of manufactured things. Dickens
is as aware as anyone in his age of the debasement of work,
of the depredations of the factory system, of the acquisitive
motive, and of the awesome power of acquired objects to
transform the very soul of man. But people in Dickens do
not buy brand-name merchandise; in fact, characters in
Dickens do not go shopping at all. Although they live, most
of them, in a highly commercialized London, they do not
read advertisements. They do not respond to newspapers
except to read headlines for melodramatic purposes. Although Dickens shows the influence of mass entertainment, his characters do not; they do not chatter on about

music-hall celebrities in the way people now talk about last night's television shows, although people in Victorian England surely did just that. Or take Hardy for a different imagination but a parallel case. No one in Victorian England was more aware than he of the transformation in much of England from an agricultural world with traditional folk values to a commercial world held together by the cash nexus. Yet he does not image forth in his fiction, any more than Dickens does, the multitudinous objects of that new world. It is, of course, not my intention to fault the Victorian novelists, only to express surprise that it seems to have taken as long as it did for novelists to learn how to make a fictional world that registers a kind of phenomenology of mass culture.

I suggest Joyce's *Ulysses* as a convenient base for considering the movement from the nineteenth century to the modernist period. Readers of Joyce will recall that people in his novel do, in fact, buy brand-name merchandise. People in *Ulysses* buy Plumtree's Potted Meat, and Joyce himself was so fascinated with the name and the product that he used it as a motif: the name appears dozens of times in the course of the book. Readers of Joyce recall that people do, in fact, read newspapers, that the multiplex stuff of a modern newspaper runs through the novel: world events, obituaries, gossip and scandal, editorial opinion, jingoistic posturing, stance-taking of all kinds, and advertisements. Readers of Joyce recall that Leopold Bloom is an advertising canvasser, that he is not only a consumer, upon whose consciousness registers the running thoughts of a mass man, but also a maker and seller of the imagery of mass culture.

In Joyce the *made* coexists with the *born*, the *well-made* with the *schlock*, the *classic* with the *disposable*; and they are all rooted in a complicated tradition that extends from ancient roots to last week's events. Unlike Flaubert, who despises the banality of the bourgeois world he shows us, Joyce embraces his world, banality and all. Surely there are different pleasures, for Joyce and anyone else, in quoting Shakespeare and quoting music-hall doggerel. And there is some legitimate sense in which the latter is banal, tasteless, and trashy, as Joyce would concede. But Joyce likes those music-hall lyrics, remembers them with fondness, lays them before us with nothing of the patent contempt of Flaubert; and it would surprise no one to discover that Joyce was personally fond of Plumtree's Potted Meat. So it is that that older tradition of the realistic novel, with its base of frustrated desire, perverted will, and human corruption, all worked out in a largely junk-free world, is faded, replaced, in the twenties and thirties, by a novel imposed upon a background of cultural objects, most of which are vulgar and devoid of merit, but few of which are despised with the hearty loathing that Flaubert gave to the basic data of his fictional world.

Why the entry of what we have come to call mass culture into the texture of the art novel occurred when it did, and why it occurred at all are questions to some extent beyond analysis. But I would suggest one relevant development in Western consciousness. The anthropologist Edmund Carpenter has pointed out how the reality of possessions for modern man often comes, not from buying, owning, and using them, but from fulfilling their advertisements: people who own products for which they have seen no advertisements feel virtually as if they do not own those products at all. An object for which one knows the advertisement, however, becomes more than a function, more than a sensory object; it becomes a luminous polarity for the conscious mind, full of nuances and satisfactions.[2] So it is that in the world of Joyce, or, for an American equivalent,

[2]*Oh, What a Blow That Phantom Gave Me!* (New York: Holt, Rinehart & Winston, 1973), p. 6.

the world of Dos Passos, the entry of mass culture into the most sophisticated of fictions is often an entry of the advertisements *for* mass culture. And so it is that the fiction of the twenties and thirties begins to respond not merely to the growth of mass culture but to the manipulated consciousness *of* mass culture that results from the new power of mass advertising.

Of the fiction of the last twenty years, a rich sense of the possibilities of cultural junk plays across both the realists and the experimentalists. In realistic fiction, such as early Roth and Updike, or in a large number of lesser known recent novels like *Bijou* by David Madden, a large amount of the solidity of the realism is made up, precisely, of cultural junk: old movies, radio serials, brand names, advertising jingles. I turn idly through Updike's *Rabbit Redux* and find references to the black go-go dancer in *Laugh-In*, David Frost, *The Match Game*, TV dinners, Carol Burnett, Gomer Pyle, the Lone Ranger, Tonto, Wheaties, McDonald's, Mobil gas, Vitalis. It is a marvelously evocative base of details, fixing the action of the novel in its appropriate place and cultural milieu. For all the differences between Joyce and contemporary realistic fiction, the use of such cultural junk is remarkably similar. In both there is an obsessive accuracy and precision. In both, the details begin to become dated almost immediately. In both there is an ambivalence of value that hovers over the details—fascination and repulsion, a full recognition of the mindless banality of that commercial trash and a nostalgic fondness for it, that ambiguity of value being a quality both of the author's imagination and our response.

Moving from the realists, however, to those kinds of recent fiction that seem to us nontraditional, suprarealistic, postmodernist, and experimental, a change occurs that is as dramatic as the change from the anger of Flaubert at the corruption of the world to the neutral assimilation of cultural junk into the fictional world of Joyce. The place to begin, in considering the relation of dreck to the concerns of recent fiction, is with Donald Barthelme, the writer who represents, in his own memorable phrase, a phrase perpetuated by William Gass, "the leading edge of the trash phenomenon." I quote a paragraph from a story by Barthelme called "City Life."

> Everybody in the city was watching a movie about an Indian village menaced by a tiger. Only Wendell Corey stood between the village and the tiger. Furthermore Wendell Corey had dropped his rifle—or rather the tiger had knocked it out of his hands—and was left with only his knife. In addition, the tiger had Wendell Corey's left arm in his mouth up to the shoulder.[3]

Judging from the summary, the movie described is a Grade B thriller, a fourth-rate jungle epic of no distinction whatever. (A friend tells me that the film referred to is *Man-Eater of Kumaon* (1948), directed by Byron Haskin, starring Sabu, Wendell Corey, Joy Ann Page, Morris Carnovsky, and Argentina Brunetti.)

The summary of the movie in Barthelme is not background, not a part of a realistic texture against which the main action is presented. Background and foreground, in fact, become meaningless terms in Barthelme. There is nothing before that ridiculous movie, nothing after it. Nothing causes, nothing results from it. Nobody in particular has made the movie, except for Wendell Corey, and nobody in particular—Barthelme says "everybody"—is watching it. The movie is not exactly foreground. But it is no longer background, as such a piece of cultural junk would be in Joyce, Updike, or a thousand novelists in the realistic tradition. Nothing is more important to keep in mind about junk in postmodernist fiction than this fact,

[3] *City Life* (New York: Bantam, 1971), p. 178.

that it has moved forward in the perspective of the novel, is no longer like designs in the wallpaper, but is like a presence in the middle of the room.

The narration of Barthelme's story describes the movie in a way that can only be called naïve, childlike, and undiscriminating. One of the effects of such narration is to eliminate any possibility of judgment: nothing in the description, not even the slightest connotation, suggests that it is a bad movie. That naïve and value-free narration becomes an indirect way, for Barthelme, of suggesting that a banal and tasteless movie need not be experienced as a banal and tasteless movie, need not be presented as such, need not be judged at all. Implicitly, Barthelme finds the movie oddly ingratiating, partly because it is so blatantly and audaciously tasteless. Analyses of *camp* tastes have diminished in the more than ten years since Susan Sontag gave the term its currency, and the word has all but disappeared; but the phenomenon remains. Perhaps we talk about it less because we all participate in it more, and what seemed perverse and clever in Susan Sontag's analysis seems largely shared and commonplace now. Barthelme's implicit attitude, in any case, has relationships to what we used to call camp taste; yet in the story the passage becomes far more than a camp reference, becoming, instead, an epistemological gesture, not simply a pointing at an object but a way of apprehending the world.

Details in fiction have always had the function of making the world of the novel seem familiar and recognizable. When we say of a novel that it is realistic, we mean that the accumulated details of its narration convince us of the authenticity of the reported experience in the novel. "Had I been there," we say as we read, "that is the way the world would have looked to me." But in Barthelme the effect is the opposite, to take a detail that we are prepared to accept as realistic, even commonplace and banal, and give it a treatment and an emphasis that make it seem strange and ridiculous. Yet, for all its strangeness, the appropriate response, I think, is an amused recognition of kinship with the experience described. Joyce's dreck is dreck remembered, arranged, understood, and aesthetically deployed. Barthelme's narrator does not *remember dreck*: he *is in the world of dreck*, a placement the reader is encouraged to share. Joyce's best readers are those who were not alive in the Dublin of 1904. Barthelme's best readers are those, bored, idle, insomniac, or moved only by an unaccountable reflex action, who do habitually flip on a tasteless old movie.

For the sake of range, I will lay out some examples from elsewhere. Kurt Vonnegut, in *Breakfast of Champions*, describes a Colonel Sanders Kentucky Fried Chicken franchise. "A chicken," he writes, "was a flightless bird which looked like this:" (here he inserts a drawing of a chicken, in the manner of a child's coloring book, done evidently by Vonnegut himself with a felt-tipped pen). "The idea," he continues, "was to kill it and pull out all its feathers, and cut off its head and feet and scoop out its internal organs— and then chop it into pieces and fry the pieces and put the pieces in a waxed paper bucket with a lid on it, so it looked like this:" (here Vonnegut draws a picture of a bucket of fried chicken). Obviously somewhat different purposes are being served in Vonnegut's novel and Barthelme's story. But the junk is the same, naïvely narrated, without cause or consequence, an aspect no longer of the background, with a mixed sense both of utter tastelessness and a bizarre kind of appeal, utterly familiar yet slightly unreal in the telling, commonplace and ignorable, yet comic. Robert Coover begins a story entitled "Panel Game": "Situation: television panel game, live audience. Stage strobelit and cameras intersecting about. Moderator, bag shape corseted and black suited, behind desk-rostrum, blinking mock-modestly at lens and lamps, practiced pucker on his soft mouth and brows arched in mild goodguy astonishment. Opposite him, the panel." Again, Coover's purposes are not identical with Barthelme's or Vonnegut's. But the junk is the same, front and center in the fiction, told in such a way as to make the episode seem very like a rerun of *What's My Line*, yet told in such a way as to make the episode seem fantastic, dreamlike, and oddly comic.

The most dazzling display of the kinds of details I have been describing is in Thomas Pynchon's *Gravity's Rainbow*. I merely point, without comment, at some of the details that play across several representative pages: The Pause That Refreshes, Moxie (by which is meant, I assume from the context, a brand of soft drink still sold in parts of the United States), Baby Ruth, an early Kelvinator refrigerator still called by its owners an "ice box," the old radio commercial for United Fruit in which Chiquita Banana cautions us against putting bananas in the refrigerator, the look of Chiquita Banana in the magazine ads with a huge hat made of fruit, the Spike Jones record from early World War II days titled "Right in the Führer's Face," the facial configurations of Japanese fighter pilots in World War II movies, the movie actor William Bendix, a violin cadenza from a concerto by Rossini, a mass parachute jump by the 82d Airborne Division, a popularized version of the Rossini violin cadenza played by a guitar-playing singer with a wiggling pelvis, the actress Fay Wray, the actress Norma Shearer, the actress Margaret O'Brien, Gimbel's basement, Frank Sinatra, Post Toasties, the shooting of John Dillinger outside the Biograph Theater, Plasticman.

A certain code or pattern lies behind the use of the fictional details whose history I have attempted to sketch. The code depends upon the intersection of three forces. The first is a linguistic force, by means of which names, words, and syntactic structures exert their own comic energy, carrying a foregrounded, attention-getting quality, a measure of grotesqueness or oddity. This, of course, is hardly an aspect peculiar to recent fiction. When Dickens names a character Mr. Fezziwig, we laugh before we find out what Mr. Fezziwig does. The second is a historical and cultural force, by means of which associations of age and obsolescence, chicness and novelty, the timeless and the dated, cultural centrality and marginality, popularity and elite exclusivity all bear on the comic effect. The third is an evaluative force, by means of which a sense of eccentric value and patent worthlessness are at once brought into play. And this peculiar evaluative force, a consistent ambivalence toward the things of the world turned toward comic purposes, is, as I have tried to sketch in the earlier portion of this chapter, new in postmodernist fiction.

I suggest a range of possibilities as a way into that code. Let us imagine a character in a novel, in the middle station of life, proper, ambitious, conventional, suburban, slightly banal. At a certain point, as a nonessential, ancillary detail, by way of accompanying an episode in his characteristic but private life, the novelist describes him eating something, between meals, as a snack. A ham sandwich, which he makes himself, from some boiled ham in the refrigerator, is, whatever else it may be, not funny. A peanut butter and jelly sandwich is slightly eccentric, or childish perhaps, but not funny. A peanut butter and jelly sandwich made with Skippy peanut butter is nearer to being funny. Half a box of Cheese TidBits is almost funny. A Clark Bar is almost funny. An Almond Joy is mildly funny. So is a box of Raisinettes, or a box of Jujubes. A Hostess Twinkie is funny.

There is, in some sense, an imagined, intended clientele for every advertised product in modern culture. That clientele may be more or less universal: surely the intent in naming many products is to stimulate the largest possible clientele although the intent in the case of others is to create an artifically restricted group to which the consumer wishes to belong. The moment something is named, much less advertised, its universality is diminished, sometimes deliberately, sometimes in ways even the cleverest advertiser cannot control. There are those who would not wish to smoke Pall Malls or wear Hush Puppies because the name of the product, in some magic and indescribable way, does not speak to them or seem to include them in its clientele. Our dailiness is filled with made objects, each with a rich and evocative name. And our half-conscious life is filled with trying out, accepting, or rejecting those names.

I suggest that it would be amusing, first, for a proper, middle-class, middle-aged, conventional character to eat a Hostess Twinkie because the name, never mind the product, does not seem to fit. Inserted into the life of such a character, the product's name has the effect of a pasted object in a collage. It startles the mind, calls attention to itself, intrigues us by its discontinuity with the rest of our field of attention. It would be amusing, secondly, because of the apparent value of the product, a bland, mass-produced sponge cake, individually wrapped, intended mainly, one supposes, for children's lunches, filled with a synthetic cream, again, in a word, dreck. In this case, the specificity of the brand name clearly has something to do with the comic effect. Clearly the abruptness of the presentation has something to do with it; if we are prepared by the novelist to respond to a plausible character who has an explainable taste for mass-produced cakes, the use of the name is no longer comic, except in a broad and diffuse way. Clearly the continuity of reference with our own world has something to do with the comic effect: it is appropriate that we recall the thing named, not merely as an object in the world, but as an object from our own experience, acknowledged with silent amusement repressed because of decorum. Most people have eaten a Hostess Twinkie and some will do so again.

Naming the Hostess Twinkie is, in some respects, a classic maneuver. It exposes a slice of the character's private life, unmasking him, middle brow though he may be, as, in unguarded moments, a lover of mass-produced sponge cakes. And it gives us a linguistic jolt, the idiotic trade name existing in a setting of well-made prose. That, too, is a classic strategy. In the twentieth century, S. J. Perelman has been making comedy out of such stylistic shifts since before most of the practitioners of experimental fiction were born. But when such a name is one element in what turns out to be an assemblage of such elements, the effect is, at the same time, comic and experimental, building upon our sense of conventional comic appeals but also willing into existence a form that is not a vehicle in which those comic events can intermittently occur but a texture that is made up of those comic events, in which the very fabric of the form is dreck.

I have chosen the easiest example of dreck to analyze, the named product, in which the name itself cannot be spoken by a reasonable man without its being automatically foregrounded, the product being both mass-produced and unique, tasteless and unaccountably palatable. Other kinds of cultural scraps are not necessarily subject to the same analysis. Barthelme's "The Indian Uprising," for example, contains, among a multitude of examples, Gabriel Fauré, a coffee table made from a hollow core door, Korzybski, Bordentown, New Jersey, Jean-Luc Godard. Still, I have promised a code by means of which such elements can be seen as parts of a pattern, notes toward a grammar, as it were, of dreck. The way to make a start at such a code is by a series of categorical generalizations, none of which is wholly true but all of which are mostly true.

An object, alone, is potentially funny when it is named if it evokes a small but real commitment of the past that the reader has long since transcended and the writer knows the reader has transcended, the object being still remembered with a fondness that is at once nostalgic and embarrassed. The brightly colored stamps from such countries as Monaco and Mozambique from one's childhood stamp collection, Fleer's bubble gum, Winnie the Pooh, Eskimo Pies.

An object, alone, is potentially funny when it is named if the naming of it suggests an unusual degree of attention being given to a small, ignorable part of the flux of disposable object, such as a third-rate actor in a forgotten film or an ignorable brand name. George Brent, Keefe Braselle, Vick's Vaporub, Shinola.

An object, alone, is potentially funny when it is named if the naming of it suggests a banal, tasteless, mass-produced quality that all of those bright enough to be reading the reference would recognize, along with a secret charm, value, or durability, so that naming the object serves to suggest the possibility of a covert indulgence shared by writer and reader. Hydrox Cookies, McDonald's hamburgers, Farah slacks, Bic ball-point pens.

An object, alone, is potentially funny when it is named if the naming of it compels the writer to reproduce the end result of an advertising campaign that necessarily has promised more power or gratification or ecstasy than the product can possibly deliver. The Plymouth Baracuda, Wheaties: Breakfast of Champions, Tabu perfume.

An object, alone, is potentially funny when it is named if the naming of it accomplishes a literalization, so that the metaphorical attributes of the product are imagined to be literally true. Tabu perfume is doubly amusing if one can imagine having to ask for it in a furtive whisper, receive it under the counter, pay for it surreptitiously, take it home in a plain brown bag. In a Barthelme story, a character wants to become an Untouchable, presumably in imitation of the police series that ran for several seasons on television, but somebody spoils his imagined ambition by touching him.

An object, alone, is potentially funny when it is named if the naming of it suggests a banal and tasteless quality that all of those bright enough to be reading the reference would recognize, but along with the banal and tasteless quality a certain flair and audacity that gives the object the special energy that used to be called "camp." A cocktail lounge located on U.S. Route 1 midway between Philadelphia and Trenton, made from a converted DC-3 airplane, an early James Cagney movie with a prison scene.

An object, alone, is potentially funny when it is named if the naming of it identifies a particular kind of cult object. The transaction between writer and reader, in this case, is almost impossibly complicated. The writer cannot know the relation of his reader to a given cult; and the reader will respond in different ways, according to his commitment to the cult. In general, the relationships operate in this way. A writer can cite a detail associated with a cult to which he expects few if any of his readers will have a commitment, an astrological chart, a framed picture of Father Divine, a copy of *Awake*, and the reader will respond with amused condescension, in ways not different from response to classic satire. A writer can cite a detail associated with a cult which he expects will be known by most of his readers, at a distance by some of them, with a degree of commitment by others, with fervent and total involvement by still others—Elaine's restaurant, the novels of Ronald Firbank, Godard's films, the literary criticism of Ronald Barthes, Coors beer. Most of those who are members of the cult will be aware of the fragility of the cult and be both amused and embarrassed to see the name of the cult object printed, foregrounded, set in a fiction. Most of those who are not members of the cult will be aware of the cult's potency and its claim to our attention, also aware of the specious fashionability of its membership, and will therefore be amused and startled to see the cult object named in a fiction.

An object, alone, is potentially funny when it is named if the naming of it revives the memory of something obsolescent, preferably with a certain mythic aura about it, toward which our moral and emotional response has changed almost beyond recall. A French tickler, spats, any song by Stephen Foster.

A series or collocation of objects is potentially funny when it is named if the naming of it suggests an encyclopedic, enumerative, obsessively assimilative energy somewhat out of control. This is, of course, an old source for comic effects, at least as old as Rabelais. But the implications of the obsessive series change from time to time. In other periods, the effect has usually been directed toward the undermining of decorum in the interest of registering the richness and multiplicity of experience. In the fiction of the present time, such apparently obsessive serializing very often registers the ambivalent response to the junk of the world I have tried to describe, an enumeration of the contents of somebody's medicine cabinet, for example, or the contents of a drugstore, as the speaker of Stanley Elkin's *The Dick Gibson Show* so manically and irrepressibly enumerates it.

> You know what a drugstore is? A temple to the senses.
> Come down those crowded aisles. Cosmetics first stop.
> Powders, puffs, a verb-wheel of polished nails on a cardboard, lipstick ballistics, creams and tighteners, suntan lotions, eyeshadow, dyes for hair—love potions, paints . . .
> shampoos, all the lotions and hair conditioners proteined as
> egg and meat . . . sun lamps, sleep masks, rollers . . . the

Venus Folding Feminine Syringe . . . supporters, rupture's
ribbons and organ's bows . . . diarrhea's plugs and consti-
pation's triggers.[4]

A word, a phrase, or a linguistic construct is potentially
funny if it suggests a slight time lag in the adoption of a
cant, chic vocabulary. To use the word *existential* more or
less gratuitously now is hardly funny because the word is
out of fashion, and a character in a fiction who uses it will
seem either a crude burlesque or a bore. But a character
in a fiction who drops a reference to the *Tel Quel* school of
French literary criticism will seem more appropriately
comic since his attempt at chic is not passé by two decades
but by two or three years.

A word, a phrase, or a linguistic construct is potentially
funny if it suggests an abortive attempt by a member of one
speech community to communicate with a member of another speech community by mimicking a device of his dialect—a white who attempts black street talk, a middle-
aged parent who attempts adolescent slang.

A word, a phrase, or a linguistic construct is potentially
funny if it suggests the special stamp of another writer, so
that its use creates a passing moment of parody. Hemingway and James can be mimicked in a phrase. And anybody
with a good ear can integrate a passing, parodic quote, recognizable and funny, from a hundred living figures from
R. D. Laing to Julia Child.

The permutations and categories of my subject are larger
than I can exhaust. But the code emerges. Each of the
categories I have proposed reinforces my initial assertion,
that the humor of dreck depends upon the simultaneous
interaction of a linguistic force, by means of which verbal
elements carry a certain foregrounded, stylized, extrava-
gant quality that inheres in the words qua words, a histori-

[4](New York: Random House, 1971), p. 184.

cal-cultural force, by means of which the vitality and obsolescence, centrality, and eccentricity of an object are suggested, and an evaluative force, in which the worth of an object is ambivalently implied. Almost everything in the world is capable of becoming trash or capable of being seen as trash. But not all of that real and potential trash is capable of being used as elements in a fiction of the kind now written by postrealistic writers, because most of the real and potential trash will merely lie there on the page, without the intricacy of intention and response that redeems that trash as art and transforms it into comedy.

A remarkable number of tendencies have converged in the seventies to produce a fiction that is unconventional and strikingly antirealistic but, at the same time, evocative of the shared perceptions of the individual in mass society, a fiction, moreover, that is formally intricate and thoroughly serious about its status as art but is funny. One tendency is simply the inevitable turn that art of any kind takes when its modes and sensibilities seem worked out and uncongenial, in this case a shift from the problematic intensity, the self-seriousness, the sheer difficulty of the modernists to the nonproblematic "fabulation" of the postmodernists, or, to put the shift another way, from the ironic and distanced voice of the modernists to the naïve, involved, vulnerable voice of the postmodernists, or, to put it still differently, from the symbolic resonance and the multileveled depth of reference of the modernists to the fascination with surface in the postmodernists.

The junk of current fiction represents a new way, also, of giving fictional specificity to a meaningless quality of life. One recalls how hard earlier writers worked to evoke a spirit of hollowness and emptiness in modern life, all of the labored naturalism of Dos Passos, for example, or Marlow's journey to the heart of darkness, which is a voyage to the heart of absurdity, in the dense and devious prose of Conrad. How natural it now is, on the other hand, to suggest those qualities of disconnection and the absence of significance by making a fiction out of pop images, free floating, without context, a set of images that allows, in some marvelous equipoise, the coexistence of an appalling view of the meaninglessness of the world along with a sense of wit and play which makes that meaningless quality bearable and often very funny.

The centrality of dreck, moreover, suggests that writers of recent fiction recognize a new audience, an audience with none of the common bonds of earlier audiences for earlier fiction. It is a truism by now to point out that readers of the best new fiction do not necessarily share common social assumptions, as readers of Victorian three-volume novels tended to do, or metaphysical assumptions, as readers of naturalistic novels tended to do. We do not share a common education, as readers of French novels have always tended to do, or a common susceptibility to certain stylistic effects, as readers of Scott or Thackeray tended to do, or a common interest in myth, as Joyce could assume of his readers. What most of us do share, along with an interest in wit, nuance, verbal play, the power and perversity of language, is a common mass culture, the central object of attention of our misspent youths, giving us a shared experience filled with trivial and nearly forgotten movies, comics, radio and television series, and a whole range of public names, events, and faces known only as their contrived and stylized images have filtered down to us through the cultural media.

The use of junk furthermore means that fiction has re-energized itself by borrowing from the vulgar arts, as fiction often has done when its best writers see its possibilities turned toward ever narrower circles of self-imitation. Fiction from the Elizabethans to Defoe energized itself by superimposing upon romance the bad taste of true crime stories. Jane Austen energized her fiction by assimilating and ironizing melodrama. Melville and Conrad energized their works by borrowing from, and then transforming, a vacuous tradition of sea fiction. And when Twain is very good, it is because he has put to his own uses the frontier tall tale. It is a process that critics have sometimes called rebarbarization, the constant renewal of serious art by borrowing from the vulgar arts. That such a process happens with somewhat more rapidity and intensity than it used to need hardly surprise us.

Finally, it happens that the use of dreck is particularly suited to a formal tendency that I have elsewhere described as verbal collage. Not all visual collages incorporate fragments of transitory value from mass culture, but very many of them do. A narrative structure that is analogous to visual collage opens itself to the assimilation of junk more readily than narrative has ever done. And a narrative structure that is analogous to Harold Rosenberg's "anxious object" opens itself to a range of comic effects that are powerfully rooted in our own uneasy time but that few of our classic descriptions of the comic have prepared us for.

CHAPTER TEN

Epilogue
Ebịoꙅᴎɘ

NEW DIRECTIONS in the art of the last century and a half have generally been surrounded with the appearance of social "agonism" (consider Spender's title *The Struggle of the Modern*, the sense at least since Wordsworth and commonplace in our time that one's own art is a counterforce, in combat with the torpor and stupidity of one's own time) and a defensive verbalism, in which the legitimacy of the new art has been described in a never-ending "introduction." Every generation of poets since Wordsworth has claimed to be writing the language actually used by men, in contrast to its lumpish and stilted predecessors. Every generation of novelists has claimed to be in touch with reality in a way denied its predecessors. These defensive maneuvers loom so large that it would not be surprising to find a reader who recalled "Tradition and the Individual Talent" as clearly as *The Wasteland*, who relished Shaw's introductions more than the plays themselves, and who recalled that there was once such a thing as vorticism without being able to name a single literary work that was in any way related to it. Of recent nontraditional fiction, however, there is not much sense of social agonism: writers like Heller, Barth, and Vonnegut are lionized. As for the manifestoes, the polemical introductions, and the defensive stance-taking so commonplace in the past, they are all virtually nonexistent. There has probably not been a comparable body of writing since the Romantic period in which the writers themselves have told us so little about what was wrong with their predecessors, how they hoped to improve upon them, and why we ought to be reading their works.

In the absence of tactical statements by the writers themselves, we can map out areas of coherence in literary history in a number of ways. One is by finding a commanding, charismatic figure who seems to have dominated the art of his time, allowing the figure's dominance to provide the center of that coherence. The Age of Pope is defined by defining both the nature of Pope's genius and the nature of his dominance. Southern Gothic fiction is ordinarily understood by fixing Faulkner at its origins and its center. Of the various writers I have cited throughout the previous chapters, one might guess that they all tend to share certain affinities (for Beckett and Kafka, perhaps for Céline and Nathanael West, or among older writers for Sterne and Rabelais); yet in their own time, the writers I cite are not dominated by anybody. There is no peak to the pyramid, and our search for that kind of coherence is pointless.

Another way of finding coherence is to discover a common ideology. The Oxford Movement is defined by what its members believed. So is the Aesthetic Movement. And our habit of grouping writers according to decade or generation is based on the assumption that writers grouped in that way can be seen to cohere by reason of their shared assumptions about the nature of the world. Of the writers I have cited, ideology may mean something in the case of Pynchon; but if it does, that peculiar entropic vision of the world seems not at all shared, at least in its particulars, by anybody else. Of Barth, *End of the Road* might plausibly be said to be expressive of an ideology, but *Chimera* surely is not. And of most of the writers I cite—Coover, Elkin, Gass, Barthelme—although they obviously value some things and deplore others, the idea of extracting a common, shared ideology from their work seems a perversion of the nature of their fiction.

Still another way of defining literary coherence is to look at the aesthetic transaction itself. We have a movement or a school when we can point to a coherent audience or a specific group of periodicals or publishers especially receptive to a specialized kind of art. The nature of *The Yellow Book*, its contributors, and its audience all cohere as a unit. And we naturally seek to understand Southern Agrarianism or the New Criticism by understanding the journals, such as the *Sewanee* and *Kenyon Reviews,* in which those aesthetic and intellectual transactions were presented. But, again, of the writers I cite there is no coherence at all. The audience for Coover does not necessarily overlap with the audience for Leonard Michaels. There is no reason why readers of Barth should also be readers of Stanley Elkin. Both Pynchon and Vonnegut generate, in different ways, cult responses; and readers of both of them often read no other contemporary fiction. No single journal stands at the center of postrealist fiction. No major publishing house is broadly responsive to it. And it is even difficult to find a book store in which a strong, representative selection of new fiction can be found. The case of Barthelme is representative of such an absence of coherence. *City Life* is made up of work published in the *New Yorker* and *Paris Review*; as a book, *City Life* was reviewed as an avant-garde mystification—and was offered as an alternate to the members of the Book-of-the-Month Club; I bought my copy from the revolving rack at a drugstore. In short, almost all of the equipment that we have for defining a direction in the history of art, setting it off from what has gone before and what comes after, breaks down in the face of those writers whom we would easily call nontraditional, an incongruous and highly individual lot.

On the other hand, the correspondences among writers of new fiction suggest, as much as the differences between them, why it is that new fiction is so little understood. *Postmodernist* is an epithet that I, for one, find annoying and unhelpful, even though I lapse into its use from time to time. But it is true, all the same, that recent fiction no longer orients itself according to its own relations to the modernist masters and that this sense of discontinuity with the dominant figures of modernism is one of the few qualities that unite new fiction. Yet criticism of fiction still derives its terms and its methods from the work of the great modernists. A professional interest in Joyce need not be exclusive of a professional interest in Coover; but, in fact, the two almost always are exclusive of each other, a fact not surprising when one reflects on the gulf in time between the two, Coover being as far in time from Joyce as Joyce is from George Eliot. What recent fiction tells us on every page is that it is of another age than the modernist masters. And what we are further obliged to recognize is that our public conceptualizing has not even acknowledged the transition, much less provided the organizing devices by means of which we can make sense of it.

There was a time when the kind of public understanding that we lack was supplied by the "man of letters." But, as John Gross has magisterially demonstrated, the man of letters has fallen and figures comparable to Henley, Saintsbury, and Middleton Murry, or more recently Edmund Wilson, are not likely to arise in our time to mediate between new art and its anxious public in a way that those older figures did. Even if such figures did exist, they would find their function difficult to perform, since new fiction tends to mock, subvert, and preempt any traditional attempts at critical interpretation of itself. And thus recent narrative art (with the exception of the "new" French novel, which has not lacked apologetics for itself) has set about creating a new set of narrative possibilities in a time when the public for fiction does not expect or wish for anybody to seek to form its taste and instruct its response and in a time when the professional interpreters of contemporary narrative art tend to be, in fact, interpreters of modernist art, which is to say the art of the half century now past.

Finally, we understand less than we should about the fiction I have attempted to describe because our modes of critical understanding are undermined by a family of metaphors to which we continue to cling with obsessive tenacity, namely the organic metaphors by which we describe the "birth," the "growth," and the "death" of fiction. Certain genres in literary history, it is true, especially the more rigid and highly specialized ones, have been ultimately abandoned; but such formal exhaustion has always been the result of a complex of causes involving audience, ideas, authorial motives, even the economics of publication and presentation. It need hardly be stressed at this point that the idea of the death of the novel has been used both tendentiously and without much sense of that complex of causes by means of which genres occasionally do die. Readers of fiction in the latter third of the eighteenth century, as J. M. S. Tompkins observes, thought the novel dead, its possibilities played out.[1] Which means that, if the novel has been dying for two centuries, there is something wrong not with the novel but with the metaphor. For a long time serious discussion of new fiction has been hobbled by the cumbersome, vacuous business of dying forms. The new fiction of the past twenty years is worth attending to on its

[1] *The Popular Novel in England,* 1770–1800 (Lincoln, Neb.: University of Nebraska Press, 1961), p. 5.

own terms, not because it is living whereas something else has died.

In the face of a body of fiction so elusive, a description that works out of a unified thesis seems to me destined to fail. There is critical work, some of it suggestive and incisive, all of it finally reductive, that attempts to locate the center of new fiction in a changed attitude toward myth, or in a shared participation in a general contemporary sensibility, or in a response toward the salient features of a preposterous public world. Old friends of mine, with their own enthusiasms, predict that a definitive structuralist study, or a definitive Marxist study, lies just over the horizon. Perhaps. But I doubt it. I would let the chapters that make up this book stand for my conviction that if one submits to new fiction and then tries to find ways of talking about it, the result is, first, a genuine amazement at the range of formal options, rhetorical stances, and angles of interaction with experience now open to writers and, second, a feeling that a kind of fluid eclecticism that opens itself to modes, styles, images, sensibilities, and rhetorical designs upon the reader is the only critical method likely, in the long run, to be true to that fiction.

From the start, I have tried to place new fiction in the tradition of previous prose fiction. The impulse now to stand back from my subject and to close the gestalt is irresistible. I have referred to the seventies as, by and large, the decade that encloses the fiction I describe, although some of the fiction that is indisputably postrealist, or postmodernist, or experimental in a contemporary sense occurs well before 1970. Obviously the idea of decades is a shorthand, and I do not think that new fiction has a kind of built-in obsolescence, fated to expire in 1980. Nor do I think that the fiction I describe has dominated the seventies in a way that my treatment of it may make it seem. I ignore Bellow in this book, although I do not ignore Bellow in my private life. I read him with enormous pleasure, and I do not imagine that I can spite the Nobel Prize committee by patronizing the comparative conventionality of his technique. The point is that the fiction of the seventies is itself a fiction; and even now, as I write this paragraph, there are surely writers of fiction executing novels to which none of my formulas apply, even novels that use technical resources hardly different from those of Balzac but are still powerful and true.

Still, the transformations that I have pointed to have happened. Much, if not all, fiction is not the same as it was. But at some point, postrealist fiction will cease to be the thing it is and will become another thing, not on December 31, 1979, but in the long run, in its own way, in its own good time. And what will happen is this.

For every trend there is a countertrend. It is surely a good guess that fiction in the eighties will tend to be less autotelic, less verbal, less playful, more mimetic, in some sense more regressive and conventional. Some readers and more than a few reviewers will applaud the trend of the most talented writers of that time away from "mere word games and virtuosity for its own sake." And it is a good guess that fiction in the eighties will find ways to revive character by finding possibilities for investing a depth and interest in individual human figures that the antirealist fiction of the present time has not sought to do. But there are certain things that will remain.

Having learned all there is to learn about hardness, dryness, and ritual despair from the classic modernists, writers of fiction are not likely again in our time to present so narrow a band of feelings as most of the fiction does before 1965. Having learned all there is to learn about ironic poise and Olympian detachment from the classic modernists, writers of fiction are not likely again in our time to imagine themselves apart from the clutter and the bad taste of the general culture. Having learned all there is to learn about investing a story with the maximum symbolic and mythic resonance, writers of fiction are not likely again in our time to go in quest of that kind of depth, having found a way to make fiction intricately and seriously superficial. Having learned what time, space, self, and other feel like in Dublin, Bloomsbury, and Nottinghamshire, the offices of the Workers' Accident Insurance Institute of Prague, the cork-lined room at 102 Boulevard Haussmann, Manhattan, and Yoknapatawpha County, writers of fiction are not likely again in our time to imagine that that peculiar kind of self-consciousness defines the contours of inner experience now. And having learned from Borges and Landolfi, Calvino and Grass, Butor and Sarraute or, having learned from Rabelais, Cervantes, and Sterne or, God knows, having learned from themselves, writers of fiction in the United States are not likely again in our time to imagine that quest novels, lyrical novels of sensibility, epiphany stories, stories of sensitive children in a Gothic world or of sensitive artists among the bourgeousie somehow exhaust the catalog of available forms.

Index

PHILIP STEVICK holds the degrees of B.A. (1955) and M.A. (1956) from Kent State University, and the Ph.D. (1963) from Ohio State University. As an outgrowth of a special interest in eighteenth- and twentieth-century fiction, he has had many essays on subjects within these areas published in the journals. He has also written three other books, *The Theory of the Novel* (1967), *The Chapter in Fiction: Theories of Narrative Division* (1970), and *Anti-Story* (1971), and has edited an edition of Richardson's *Clarissa* (1971). He is currently on the English faculty at Temple University.